The Lizard Keeper's Handbook

FROM THE EXPERTS AT
ADVANCED VIVARIUM SYSTEMS™

By Philippe de Vosjoli

THE HERPETOCULTURAL LIBRARY™
Advanced Vivarium Systems™
Irvine, California

Karla Austin, *Director of Operations and Product Development*
Nick Clemente, *Special Consultant*
Barbara Kimmel, *Managing Editor*
Jessica Knott, *Production Supervisor*
Joe Bernier, *Designer*
Cover and layout design concept by Michael Capozzi
Indexed by Melody England

Front and back cover photos by Paul Freed.
Paul Freed: 11, 16, 19, 20, 22, 23, 26, 28, 31, 34, 37, 40–42, 44–46, 51, 53, 54, 57, 59, 60–64, 67, 68, 70–72, 83, 88, 101, 109–112, 114, 116, 135, 140, 148, 157, 159, 161, 163, 166–171, 173–187. Roger Klingenberg: 75, 76, 93, 97, 126, 138, 141, 144, 146, 147, 149–153. Bill Love: 7, 8, 13, 17, 21, 25, 33, 39, 52, 56, 102, 104, 107, 115, 117, 121, 131, 136, 164, 165

Copyright © 2007 by Advanced Vivarium Systems™

All rights reserved. No part of this book may be reproduced, stored in a retrieval system, or transmitted in any form or by any means, electronic, mechanical, photocopying, recording, or otherwise, without the prior written permission of Advanced Vivarium Systems™, except for the inclusion of brief quotations in an acknowledged review.

LCCN: 96-183295
ISBN: 978-1-882770-96-0

An Imprint of BowTie Press®
A Division of BowTie, Inc.
3 Burroughs
Irvine, CA 92618
866-888-5526

Printed and bound in Singapore
1 2 3 4 5 6 7 8 9 10
12 11 10 09 08 07

CONTENTS

FOREWORD

When I wrote the original *Lizard Keeper's Handbook* in 1994, my goal was to provide beginning hobbyists with the concepts that I considered to be essential knowledge for good keepers. Since then, the rise of the Internet has changed the hobby dramatically: on one hand, spreading some important information; on the other hand, contributing to the dumbing down of the hobby. Instead of introducing the public to the rich ecology of ideas associated with reptile keeping, the current trend on the Internet is quickie answers about the care of newly acquired pets. This information is usually disseminated through posting on one of the many online reptile forums now available. However, few lizards have simple enough requirements to fare well when their keepers follow simple formulas without giving thought to the many factors that contribute to success or failure. To my surprise, many beginner lizard keepers no longer bother learning the scientific names of their pets or their pets' geographical origins.

In-depth information is one of the great advantages of books. Books often provide more information than you bargained for and consequently help expand the limits of your awareness. I have found that the field of herpetoculture becomes more complex and consequently more fascinating with daily lessons that lead to a more enlightened philosophy of life.

In terms of the herpetoculture of reptiles, the keeping of lizards is probably the most challenging. Lizards demonstrate a great diversity of adaptations and specializations. In addition, the habits of smaller species, unlike those of most snakes and turtles, make them ideal candidates to keep and display in naturalistic vivaria. Utilizing naturalistic vivaria adds landscaping and horticulture to the hobby, raising it to the level of an art form. Aesthetic compositions are created by combining live plants and natural materials, such as wood and rock.

In this updated version of the handbook, I decided to add new essential concepts that I developed with my friends Susan Donoghue, VMD, and Roger Klingenberg, DVM, in the course of coauthoring a series of articles that appeared in *Vivarium Magazine* in 1999 on the Multifactorial Model of Herpetoculture. This model explains how the health, welfare, and fecundity of a species are the result of several interacting factors such as age, temperature, and diet that can vary within certain parameters and still lead to success. One reason for this inclusion was to oppose a new righteousness that seems to have emerged in Internet forums by self-made overnight authorities. These so-called experts parrot the work of others and make indignant claims against those who do not follow their husbandry formulas. Almost a half century of reptile keeping has made me more humble and aware that there can be several ways to successfully keep a species. This is the basis of a multifactorial model. For example, the type of diet and supplementation provided a reptile will determine whether a UVB source is required or not. The temperature gradients will determine growth and maturity rates, but both will also be affected by diet and social factors.

Although the field of herpetoculture has made great progress in recent years, it is still in its infancy. Many of the neat, beautiful, most mind-boggling lizards (e.g., most true chameleons and tree dragons of the genus *Gonocephalus*) have yet to be established in captivity. There remains much innovation to explore. There is also great ground to cover to assure that a direct experience with these species, made possible through herpetoculture, remains available to human societies. The conservation of a diversity of reptile-human interface through responsible care and captive propagation is the primary goal of herpetoculture and a legacy we hopefully will leave for future generations.

Because herpetoculture is rapidly expanding, new information is becoming available every year. Some of this information will make a significant portion of our current knowledge obsolete. Ongoing research on lizard diets and nutrition will result in new approaches to feeding lizards and insects and the development of better vitamin and mineral supplements. Because of this rapidly changing base of knowledge, this manual will likely be revised over the years to include updated information.

INTRODUCTION

nsect-eating (insectivorous) lizards, an arbitrary grouping based on dietary preference, account for a great majority of the more than 3,800 recognized species of lizards. They comprise one of the most successful groups of vertebrates; they have evolved a great variety of forms and adaptations and colonized a wide diversity of habitats.

In many areas, insect-eating lizards are extremely abundant, accounting for a significant percentage of the animal biomass. Primarily because of this relative abundance, several species of insect-eating lizards are collected and sold by the thousands annually in the pet trade. Some of the most common are anoles, long-tailed lizards, skinks, and some geckos. With proper management, which should include establishing collecting seasons for respective species and annual quotas based on field studies, many of the populations of insect-eating lizards have a high recovery rate and are good candidates for sustained field culture. This method

There are many exciting insect-eating lizards now available in the pet trade.

is also called ranching, and it consists of managing populations in the wild through controlled harvesting and, to varying degrees, through reduction of predators and possibly supplemental feeding. The current philosophy in herpetoculture strives toward establishing viable, self-sustaining, captive-breeding populations through managed field culture or more controlled systems of indoor and outdoor vivaria or both. A number of lizard species, such as some of the geckos, bearded dragons, and more recently veiled chameleons, have proven very adaptable and economical to breed in large numbers in captivity.

Generally, the lizards that are easy to maintain in captivity are the species that are the most adaptable to the relatively simple setups and limited diets provided by most keepers. Species that are very specialized, either in terms of their environmental requirements or in terms of their dietary needs, require a much closer duplication of those conditions and requirements to survive in captivity. Because of the diversity of adaptations and consequent requirements of insect-eating lizards, any prospective lizard keeper will need to acquire a sound base of information on lizard husbandry, as well as basic information on the particular species to be kept. A lizard maintained under the wrong conditions and offered the wrong diet cannot survive for very long in captivity.

Leopard geckos are among the easiest to keep and most popular of available reptiles.

The purpose of this book is to give herpetoculturists, both beginners and those more experienced, as well as pet industry personnel, a broad base of knowledge that will allow them to successfully keep a variety of insect-eating lizards. Although the emphasis of this book is on husbandry, all herpetoculturists should strive to captive-breed the species they keep. This helps provide important information on the captive-breeding and -rearing of a wide variety of species; it also plays an important part in assuring that these species remain available for years to come. Remember: species that are inexpensive and readily available today can become valuable, rare, and highly in demand in the future. As a herpetoculturist, you'll find that opportunities for acquiring an important base of knowledge abound. Indeed, relatively little is known of the life history, social behaviors, husbandry requirements, and reproduction of the great majority of lizards. A continually improved base of knowledge, combined with the involvement of herpetoculturists, could one day play a critical role in the conservation of many of these species.

CHAPTER 1

OBTAINING INFORMATION ABOUT INSECT-EATING LIZARDS

I cannot overemphasize the need to acquire information about the insect-eating lizard (or any reptile) you are considering buying. Keeping lizards is very different from keeping dogs, cats, or birds, and considerably more attention needs to be given to environmental and dietary factors. Although this book offers methods for determining the requirements of most insect-eating lizards, whenever possible you should strive to obtain accurate species-specific information.

Finding Information on Your Lizard

Because different lizard species have specific requirements, it is critical that you research their care prior to purchase. Fortunately, there is now a wealth of literature on reptiles available from book dealers, specialized reptile stores, and a variety of Internet sites.

Obtain as much information as possible from the seller at the time of purchase, including the correct name of the animal and its country of origin. Whenever possible, obtain the scientific name of the animal. Common names of reptiles in the pet trade often have little resemblance to the names used by herpetologists; this may confuse your search for information. Exporters are required to list animals by scientific name, and this has become standard procedure in the mail-order reptile business. However, scientific names may sometimes be inaccurate or outdated. Once you learn the scientific name and the country or area of origin, you can search the Internet for sources of information—either sites that specialize in the group of lizards you are interested in or sources of books on herpetoculture. In addition to finding information on the Internet, buy books on the lizards you are keeping to obtain as broad a base of knowledge on the subject as possible. A number of publishers, including BowTie Press (Advanced Vivarium Systems), produce species- or family-specific books that provide most of the basic information on husbandry you will need. If you can find no information that specifically addresses the husbandry of your reptile species, some valuable guidelines can be derived from field guides and other books on the herpetology and natural history of reptiles. Although

There is plenty of information available for common lizards, such as this bearded dragon (*Pogona vitticeps*). However, information on less common lizards may take some searching.

only a few specialized reptile dealers have an extensive selection of the herpetological works available, there are many mail-order natural history book dealers who offer a good selection of reptile-related literature. Check herpeto-cultural publications such as *Reptiles*, *Reptilia*, *Reptile Care*, and herpetological society newsletters for sources. A few of the larger herpetological societies also sell a selection of herpetological books.

If you cannot locate useful information from those sources, information can often be found in the herpetological publications and books available at a local university library, particularly at universities with herpetology departments. Another course is to search through scientific literature on herpetology. For example, going to a university library and consulting the *Zoological Record*, as far back as twenty years, can produce potentially valuable references. Ask a librarian for assistance in helping you learn to use the *Zoological Record*. These sources of information, scientific articles, will yield additional sources—consult the references mentioned at the end of the article.

Common Sense

One problem with literature research is that it takes time. Because time may be at a premium when you have a newly obtained species, common sense also plays an important role in initially designing a vivarium and determining a dietary regimen.

One approach is to examine the form of an animal for clues to its habits. As an example, many flattened lizards are rock dwellers. Laterally flattened lizards with long tails are usually arboreal. The long tails provide stability for arboreal lizards when climbing and resting on branches. Lizards with vertical pupils are crepuscular (active around dawn and dusk) or nocturnal (active at night), while lizards with round pupils are usually diurnal (active during the daylight hours). Lizards with flattened snouts (shovel-nose appearance), smooth, very shiny scales, and reduced limbs are often fossorial (they bury in substrate). Lizards with toe pads, such as geckos and anoles, are climbing lizards; they

Look at your lizard for clues to its needs. Close up, you will see that this leaf-tailed gecko (*Uroplatus fimbriatus*) has toe pads, indicating that it requires branches to climb on.

climb on bark, rock, and plants. With experience, you will learn to take cues from a lizard's appearance and behavior when assessing its requirements.

When in doubt about a lizard's requirements, the easiest way to assess them is to design a vivarium rich in topographical and microclimatological diversity. This type of vivarium should include a variety of shelters, climbing areas, substrates, temperature and humidity ranges, and light. When a lizard is introduced into this type of environment, it usually chooses what it prefers. By observing the lizard's behavior, you should be able to determine its preferences. Remember that some lizards, particularly species from mountain areas, may require cooler temperatures, so allow for a cool gradient in an experimental vivarium if you suspect you may have such a species.

You may also want to experiment with diet. Several species of insect-eating lizards (day geckos, veiled chameleons, bearded dragons, and swifts) also eat some plant material and even baby foods. Others may feed on nonliving foods, such as lean canned dog food, fine strips of beef heart, or chopped boiled chicken. These may include many of the small teiids and skinks, some of the larger agamines, some of the lacertids, and small monitors. Lizards that are frequent tongue flickers often feed on nonliving food. Your observation and experimentation may prove to be the best source of information for determining your lizard's preferences. As long as an animal is healthy at the time of purchase or collection, you should have enough time to determine its requirements by experimentation. Remember that information from non-specialized or inexperienced people can often be wrong.

CHAPTER 2

THINGS TO CONSIDER BEFORE YOU BUY

Several factors should be considered before buying insect-eating lizards. Many first-time buyers make initial errors in selection that eventually result in disappointment or failure. Consider the following issues before purchasing a reptile.

Who Are the Lizards For?

Are the lizards for you or for your children? Except for the larger, easily handled species such as leopard geckos, bearded dragons, Sudan plated lizards, and Schneider's skinks, insect-eating lizards are not recommended for children unless their parents can provide close supervision. Parents must be willing to assume responsibility and supervision for proper maintenance and handling. Although lizards should not be considered children's pets, they are highly recommended for responsible adolescents.

Do You Want a Display Lizard or a Pet That Can Be Handled?

If regular handling is a consideration, then inquire about species that have an established reputation as pets, such as bearded dragons (*Pogona vitticeps*) or Sudan plated lizards (*Gerrhosaurus major*). Leopard geckos (*Eublepharis macularius*) and African fat-tail geckos (*Hemitheconyx caudicinctus*) can also be handled on occasion; however, the great majority of insect-eating lizards are best considered primarily for display.

If your new lizard is for your kids, buy something hardy and easy to care for. Leopard geckos and bearded dragons are especially good.

Other lizards outside of the insect-eating group, such as green iguanas, Australian blue-tongue skinks, and some of the monitors, are better candidates for a relatively high level of human interaction.

Avoid Buying on Impulse

Do a little research or reading on the species you are considering buying. Many impulse buyers are sorry later when they realize they can't readily accommodate the needs of their animal or if the animal doesn't meet their expectations. Their animal also may not fare well, become ill, and die. Many impulse buyers of horned lizards, true chameleons, and some of the Chilean lizards have been discouraged because they were unaware that these species tend to be difficult to keep in captivity.

Be Willing to Pay for the Appropriate Setup

Many people buying a lizard for the first time attempt to save money on essentials, such as a properly sized enclosure or adequate heating and lighting. However, you will find the cost of an adequate vivarium is usually several times the cost of the animal(s) you are purchasing. This is the same cost relationship one encounters with the tropical fish hobby. Skimping on the purchase of essentials such as a tank that will accommodate a growing animal or the right heat and light sources can end up harming the health of a new pet or make it necessary for you to spend even more in the near future.

Be willing to invest in the right vivarium for the lizard you plan to buy.

Consider Your Lizard's Feeding

You must also consider whether you will be able to adequately and regularly feed the animal(s) you purchase. With insect-eating lizards, this usually means making a once-a-week trip to a local pet store, raising your own insects, or having them delivered by mail order. Take into account the time it takes to provide an adequate diet for these lizards.

Consider Sex When Making a Selection

If you are considering buying a single lizard, a male is generally preferable to a female. In my experience, male insect-eating lizards tend to live longer in captivity than females do. In addition, females without males will not be given the opportunity to breed. If they are not bred when they are ovulating, they may have an increased chance of becoming egg-bound. The wisest decision is to buy a sexual pair or a trio (one male, two females), when possible, and to provide your animals with the opportunity to reproduce. However, keeping animals singly will eliminate social competition and is the best method if your goal is to have a show specimen.

Understand the Commercial Selection of Lizards

Many nonspecialized, relatively inexperienced pet stores base their lizard inventory more on potential profit than on how well specific lizards fare in captivity. This was the case with several types of Chilean lizards imported in the past. They were inexpensive and pretty, yet seldom survived more than a few months. Some pet store owners lack basic knowledge about reptiles and often try to minimize losses by selling cheap wild-collected species. Unfortunately, inexperienced customers who want to save money often select inexpensive wild-collected species that do not fare well in captivity. It cannot be emphasized enough: do your homework before you buy a lizard. There are specialized stores with personnel who know reptiles well; they can help you select a species that meets your specific needs. There are also many good books available and herpetoculturists who are willing to share their knowledge.

CHAPTER 3

SOME RECOMMENDED INSECT-EATING LIZARDS

There are several insect-eating lizards that do better in captivity than others. The following sections highlight those that are recommended for keepers, followed by a list of those that are difficult to keep.

Geckos (Families Eublepharidae and Gekkonidae)

Overall, this diverse group of lizards of more than 900 species is very adaptable to captivity. More species in this family are captive-bred than in any other. However, some of the terrestrial species and tropical forest species can be delicate and may need specialized care.

Leopard geckos (*Eublepharis macularius*) are now selectively bred in a variety of colors and patterns.

Some geckos rank among the most beautiful of lizards; others have bizarre and interesting forms, such as the leaf-tail geckos. Their eyes are some of the most remarkable in the animal world. Among popular favorites there are leopard geckos (*Eublepharis macularius*), African fat-tailed geckos (*Hemitheconyx*), day geckos *(Phelsuma)*, Tokay geckos *(Gecko gecko)*, flying geckos *(Ptychozoon)*, prehensile-tailed geckos (*Rhacodactylus*), and frog-eyed geckos (*Teratoscincus*).

Agamid Lizards

No generalizations can be made about agamine lizards; they comprise a very diverse group of lizards. Some species are very adaptable to captivity, such as inland bearded dragons (*Pogona vitticeps*), the clown agamas of the pet trade (*Laudakia stellio brachydactyla*), and green water dragons *(Physignathus cocincinus)*. Other species, such as members of the genera *Gonocephalus, Draco,* and *Calotes* are best recommended for specialists because of their narrow environmental constraints.

Water dragons (*Physignathus cocincinus*) adapt fairly easily to captivity.

The veiled chameleon (*Chamaeleo calyptratus*) is the easiest of all the chameleons to keep in captivity.

Some species are especially difficult, such as toad-head agamas (*Phrynocephalus*) and several species in the genus *Agama*.

True Chameleons (Family Chamaeleonidae; subfamily Chamaeleonidae)

Most true chameleon species are best considered moderately to highly difficult to keep in captivity. Even the longevity of many species in the wild is quite short. However, the veiled chameleon from Yemen (*Chamaeleo calyptratus*) has proven very adaptable to captivity and is now being bred in increasing numbers by herpetoculturists in the United States. The panther chameleon from Madagascar (*Furcifer pardalis*) has also proven quite adaptable. Major breakthroughs in the care and breeding of chameleons have recently led to increasing success with these fascinating lizards.

Basilisks (Genus *Basiliscus*)

Basilisks are generally hardy once they are established. They have a few basic requirements such as large enclosures, preferably including plants. The brown basilisk (*Basiliscus basiliscus*) and the spectacular green or double-crested basilisk (*Basiliscus plumifrons*) are now bred in some numbers.

Anoles (Genus *Anolis*)

Many species of anoles, including the popular green anole (*Anolis carolinensis*), fare well in captivity and breed regularly.

Basilisks, such as this *Basiliscus vittatus*, are generally hardy in captivity.

The green anole and the brown anole (*Anolis sagrei*) are highly recommended for beginners and display well in naturalistic vivaria. The knight anole (*Anolis equestris*), introduced into Florida from Cuba, is the largest of the genus. It is very adaptable to captivity and is regularly available. This genus has generally been neglected by American herpetoculturists because of their small size and low commercial value. However, many species make outstanding vivarium display animals.

Curly-Tailed Lizards (Genus *Leiocephalus*)
The terrestrial curly-tailed lizards (*Leiocephalus*) are generally hardy and highly recommended as vivarium lizards.

Girdle-Tailed Lizards and African Plated Lizards (Family Cordylidae and Gherrosauridae)
Members of the genera *Cordylus, Pseudocordylus,* and *Gerrhosaurus* are generally hardy captives, as are some of the larger Madagascar plated lizards (*Zonosaurus*), such as *Zonosaurus maximus* and *Zonosaurus quadrilineatus*. Some of the *Gerrhosaurus*, such as *Gerrhosaurus major*, become quite tame.

Lacertas (Family Lacertidae)

Many of the lacertids adapt very well to captivity, particularly species of *Lacerta* and *Podarcis*. Several species have been bred in captivity. Beyond making good display animals, many become tame.

Skinks (Family Scincidae)

Many species of skinks fare well in captivity if provided the proper type of vivarium. Desert-dwelling burrowers, such as ocellated skinks (*Chalcides ocellatus*) and sandfish (*Scincus scincus*), should be provided with sand to burrow in. Tropical forest skinks and temperate forest skinks should have a substrate to burrow in, as well as climbing areas of cork bark. Obtaining information on a species' habitat will be important in determining the proper vivarium design.

Legless Lizards

These are the limbless members of the family Anguidae. The two European species are easily maintained in captivity. One slow worm lizard (*Anguis fragilis*) allegedly lived in captivity to the ripe old age of fifty-four years. The largest species, the sheltopusik (*Ophisaurus apodus*) of southeastern Europe and southwestern Asia, is occasionally imported and very hardy. However, these two species should be cooled down in

Although often dismissed by hobbyists, green anoles (*Anolis carolinensis*) make excellent vivarium subjects.

the winter to do well long term. The U.S. species are somewhat more difficult to keep in captivity.

Monitor Lizards (Family Varanidae)
Smaller species of monitors are insectivorous and are occasionally offered by specialized reptile dealers. Australian ridge-tailed monitors (*Varanus acanthurus*) and other dwarf monitors are now readily available as captive-bred specimens. Green tree monitors (*Varanus prasinus*) and Timor monitors (*Varanus timorensis*), currently imported in small numbers from Indonesia, are primarily insectivorous. Nearly all the larger monitor species start off as insect-eating lizards before graduating to become vertebrate-eating carnivores.

Difficult Species
The following species are difficult to keep alive long-term in captivity and are recommended for specialists only:

- Australian moloch (*Moloch horridus*)
- Butterfly agama (*Leiolepis belliana*)
- Horned lizards (*Phrynosoma*)
- Toad-headed agamas (*Phrynocephalus*)

The following are moderately difficult and are not recommended for beginners, primarily because of their environmental requirements such as higher humidity combined with ventilation or the need for a UVB source:

- Bent-toed geckos (*Cyrtodactylus*)
- Prehensile-tailed iguanids (*Polychrus marmoratus*)
- Casque-headed lizard (*Corytophanes cristatus*)
- Tree dragons (*Gonocephalus* and *Calotes* species)
- Whip-tailed lizards (*Cnemidophorus* species)
- Many Chilean species, such as *Liolaemus*)
- True chameleons, except *Chamaeleo calyptratus* and *Furcifer pardalis*

Captive-Bred Versus Wild-Caught
Regardless of species, captive-bred lizards generally fare considerably better than wild-caught lizards because they are

When possible, always purchase captive-bred rather than wild-caught lizards.

less likely to be infested with parasites or have diseases. Indeed, captive-bred lizards that have been established over several generations have a proven history of adapting to captivity. Unfortunately, relatively few species of insect-eating lizards are currently bred on a large commercial scale. Of these, the best known are the leopard gecko (*Eublepharis macularius*) and crested gecko (*Rhacodactylus ciliatus*), possibly the easiest of all lizards to keep in captivity. The Australian inland bearded dragon (*Pogona vitticeps*), a delightful and personable species, is now being bred in increasing numbers (a few thousand annually), and its availability is expected to increase. Although bearded dragons are somewhat delicate as hatchlings, subadults and adults tend to fare well. Efforts are also being made to captive-breed the veiled chameleon (*Chamaeleo calyptratus*) on a large scale. There are many other species of insect-eating lizards that are bred on a small scale, including many kinds of geckos, basilisks, and water dragons.

The mortality of wild-collected lizards is high, particularly with species requiring specialized environments and diets. If you are just starting out with lizards, select species that are known to establish well in captivity. Starting out with difficult species often results in failure; this might discourage you from further pursuing the fascinating field of herpetoculture.

Large Lizards
Large lizards, such as basilisks, green water dragons, green tree monitors (yes, this is an insect-eating species), and

bearded dragons require relatively large enclosures, along with more extensive lighting and heating than smaller species require. Larger animals tend to damage or destroy live plants in a display and may alter the landscape. They also require more frequent maintenance compared with smaller species. Large lizards eat larger prey, more food per meal, and consequently defecate greater volumes than do smaller species.

If ease of handling is an important consideration, then a medium-to-large species, such as a leopard gecko, lacerta, Sudan plated lizard, or bearded dragon, is usually a better choice than a smaller species.

Miniature Species

Many of the smaller species of lizards have been neglected by herpetoculturists. Unfortunately, humans tend to focus initially on what stands out the most. Something big and colorful and outrageously different draws our attention away from our routine experiential repertoire. Even if you have never paid attention to reptiles before, a very large reptile will make you notice it. Indeed, large snakes and large lizards are among the best crowd-drawing displays in zoos. People often stand and stare at the animals for a long time, fascinated and sometimes even frightened.

On the other hand, miniature reptiles require a special kind of attention and often appeal to those who notice the

Don't forget about the dwarf species; they can be very fascinating. This is a Cape dwarf chameleon (*Bradypodion pumilum*).

small details of their world. Anyone who has marveled at the degree of miniaturization that can be achieved by nature, at the incredible detail of physical features, subtle color, and expression of the smallest forms of life, is in for a treat with miniature lizards (snout-to-vent length usually under 2½ inches). For those who haven't yet taken the time to notice them, spend a few minutes focusing on miniature species— a heretofore unknown aspect of the natural world may open to you. I am continually fascinated by how animals with such small brains can perform relatively complex behaviors.

The advantages of miniature species are many:

- They don't require large vivaria.
- Most miniature lizards are relatively inexpensive.
- You can keep a variety of miniature species in a relatively small space.
- Miniature lizards can be kept in naturalistic vivaria because they usually do not damage the landscape.
- The maintenance of miniature species is less demanding than that of larger species, in part because small lizards have small feces.
- Many miniature species can be kept in groups. Because of this, a wide variety of behaviors can be observed, including captive breeding.
- Some species can be mixed in a naturalistic vivarium. This can make for an outstanding display. You can house a relatively large number of animals if you keep them in a large enclosure.

Among the best species of miniature lizards are the miniature geckos (*Tropiocolotes, Stenodactylus, Gonatodes, Sphaerodactylus, Coleonyx*, some of the dwarf day geckos including *Phelsuma* and *Lygodactylus*, dwarf Australian *Diplodactylus*); the smaller species of lacertids such as *Holaspis guentheri*; several species of skinks; Utas; and the dwarf chameleons of the genera *Brookesia* and *Rhampholeon*. Many other miniature species also make excellent captives. Herpetoculturists interested in these lizards usually watch for new miniature species as they become available.

U.S. lizards, such as this collared lizard hatchling (*Crotaphytus collaris*), are often ignored by hobbyists.

At one time, the biggest challenge to keeping miniature species was finding a source for small insects; but crickets are now available in a variety of sizes, and several species of small insects can easily be raised.

North American Lizards

These lizards have been generally neglected by U.S. herpetoculturists. They may believe that these lizards are common and therefore not worth the trouble or that nonnative species are more challenging and interesting. One of the possible consequences of this short-sighted perspective is that several U.S. species may one day become unavailable to herpetoculturists. Indeed, there is currently a legislative trend, not always sound in its reasoning and implementation, toward protecting native species and restricting collection of animals from the wild. Many U.S. species are outstanding and would be greatly missed if they were no longer available to hobbyists. Some of the species that should be established as self-sustaining, captive-propagated populations include the various species and morphs of the collared lizards (*Crotaphytus*), banded geckos (*Coleonyx*), various desert spiny lizards (*Sceloporus*), desert iguanas (*Dipsosaurus dorsalis*), chuckwallas (*Sauromalus obesus*), and alligator lizards (*Elgaria* and *Gerrhonotus*). Collection of these species from the wild should be primarily for the purpose of establishing them in herpetoculture rather than for their wholesale to the pet trade.

In areas where these species occur naturally, the use of outdoor vivaria is the most recommended method for their herpetoculture.

Animal Rights Organizations

Animal rights organizations sometimes have agendas at odds with the goals of herpetoculture, including putting an end to exotic animal keeping. If you support herpetoculture and care about the conservation of biodiversity, research animal organizations before joining them. Make sure that you share the same goals. Do not confuse animal rights with animal welfare; the terms and the issues are as different as night and day (see Marquardt, et al. 1993).

CHAPTER 4

SELECTION OF INSECT-EATING LIZARDS

Your success in keeping insect-eating lizards depends on your initial selection of healthy animals. Any altruistic notions of saving that poor, skinny, ill animal in a pet store should be put out of mind immediately. Despite your best intentions, thin and sick-looking lizards generally die. If you have never kept lizards before, experiences with sick lizards are likely to discourage you. If you have other lizards, you risk introducing diseases into your collection. Only more experienced keepers with quarantine facilities should consider obtaining substandard, less-than-healthy-appearing, or thin lizards. Sometimes, because a species is very rare or seldom available, specialists obtain whatever specimens they can in an attempt to establish them in herpetoculture. However, they are fully aware of the risks involved at the outset.

Selecting a Potentially Healthy Lizard

Now that you have learned the important lesson of choosing the species of lizard that best meets your needs and desires, the next step is to select a potentially healthy animal to the best of your ability. Ideally, you should research breeders and other available sources and aim for buying high-quality animals. When possible, examine animals in person; if buying online, request photos of the specimens offered.

The following guidelines should assist you in your selection:

Whether you are looking at a group of lizards or at an individual specimen, take some time to observe the lizard(s) you are considering buying. Healthy lizards tend to be active with their eyes wide open when moving. Watch the way the lizard moves about the enclosure. Notice if something is off in its walk. Is it dragging a foot or having trouble keeping its body up off the ground? Does it gape or forcibly exhale air on a regular basis? If so, this may be a sign of respiratory infection. Observe the group. Are there a number of sick-looking animals? If so, be aware that even the healthy-appearing lizard(s) you select may have been exposed to parasites or disease.

Once you have decided on a particular animal, ask to hold it. Many pet store personnel may be reluctant to hand you a lizard. In those cases, simply ask that the animal be presented to you so that you can observe it. A healthy lizard feels solid when held in the hand; a surprisingly light lizard may be emaciated. Many lizard species squirm or struggle when held and give a clear impression of muscular vigor. In a healthy lizard, the tail is rounded or appears full if it is a species with a flattened tail. The outline of the tail bones should not be visible. A lizard with good weight has a rounded hip area. In underweight lizards, the outline of the upper surface of the hip bones and of the backbone becomes apparent; with very thin lizards, the hip bones, backbone, and sometimes ribs (e.g., in true chameleons) become very prominent. Avoid thin lizards.

Always ask to handle the lizard to assess its health before purchase.

Tail Dropping

Lizards that are very nervous and frightened, particularly geckos, may drop their tails when handled. Try to make the best judgment possible without unnecessary handling of these animals.

Examine digits and limbs and look for unusual swellings, lumps, or missing digits. Check the back and belly for limb or skin damage. Look around the vent. The anal scale(s) should lie flat against the body. There should not be any swelling or crusting, unusual depressions, or smeared feces in the vent area. Examine the sides and look for collapsed or broken ribs. In some cases, these appear as depressed areas along the side of the animal; in other cases, they appear as rather sharp projections. As a rule, broken ribs give an asymmetrical appearance to the body of a lizard and are usually quite noticeable.

Look at the head. Check that both eyes are wide open. Look for opacities (cloudiness) in the eyes. Look at the head and neck area for lumps or swelling.

Using your thumb, gently press up against the throat of the animal. Bubbly mucus emerging from the nostrils when performing this procedure indicates a respiratory infection. If the lizard opens its mouth, examine the mouth area. It should be clear of bubbly mucus or any lumps, bleeding, or caseous (cheesy-looking) matter.

Sexing

If you have any intentions of breeding lizards or if you want to keep several specimens of the same species together, it is critical that you sex the animals you are purchasing. The following is a brief outline of how to sex lizards. Clearly, this depends on there being an observable difference between animals. Fortunately, you will find this to be the case with most species offered in the pet trade.

Sexual Dimorphism

In many species, there are differences in form, size, or color that make the sexes easily recognizable. Good examples of obvious sexual dimorphism are basilisk lizards. The adult males have head crests, dorsal crests, or both, making them unmistakable.

The first step when sexing a species is to look for obvious indications of sexual dimorphism. Several examples follow:

Differences in:

- size (e.g., males are larger than females)
- color (e.g., males have orange-red heads)
- body proportions (e.g., males have larger heads or females are more heavy bodied)
- ornaments and crests (e.g., males have larger crests than females do)
- scalation (e.g., male chameleon anoles have two enlarged postanal scales. In several geckos, males have enlarged cloacal spurs)

Presence of enlarged femoral or preanal pores:

Look at the underside of many lizard species; notice the presence of pores along the underside of the thigh. The pores are often enlarged in males and reduced or

Sex can often be determined by obvious differences in the postanal area.

nearly absent in females. In some species, these enlarged pores are located just anterior to the vent and are called preanal pores. In males of the clown agama (*Laudakia stellio brachydactyla*), there is a midventral line of pores running the length of the belly. These pores secrete waxy scalelike substances (particularly during the breeding season) that are believed to be used in marking territory.

Hemipenile bulges in males:
In many species of lizards, clearly defined hemipenile bulges are visible just beyond the vent at the base of the tale. As the term implies, the hemipenile bulge is caused by the inverted hemipenes of males. Looking for hemipenile bulges is a reliable method for sexing many lizards.

Manual Eversion of Hemipenes

In some species of lizards, the differences between males and females may not be obvious. One method of sex determination that is sometimes effective, but which must be performed with extreme care so as to avoid injuring the animal, is manual eversion of hemipenes. This is done by having one

Female (left) and male (right) skinks (*Tribolonotus gracilis*) are not easily sexed by observation alone.

person hold the animal (abdomen facing up) while another rolls the thumb—applying gentle pressure with the thumb starting at an area at the base of the tail just past where the hemipenes hypothetically end—toward the vent to cause eversion of the hemipenes. In lizards, the anal plate usually needs to be lifted to perform this procedure successfully.

Manual eversion of the hemipenes should be learned from an experienced herpetoculturist or experienced reptile veterinarian. Performed in the wrong manner, it can result in a crushing-type trauma or tail loss. It is effective only with some species, notably certain species of skinks (e.g., *Mabuya* species, *Lygosoma fernandi*), and is generally ineffective with most species.

Probing

With some species that cannot readily be sexed, sexing probes are sometimes used. This requires experience and involves pulling back the anal scale(s) to better expose the vent. A small probe is inserted into one of the small openings on either side of the vent. In males of some species, the presence of inverted hemipenes allows the probe to penetrate deeper than it does in females. When present on females, the openings on the sides of the vents lead to postanal glands and do not usually allow a probe as deep as do those of males. Some males have hemipenile ridges when inverted, which cause hemipenile constrictions that make probing and accurate sex determination difficult. This procedure also needs to be learned from an experienced herpetoculturist or experienced reptile veterinarian. Because most insect-eating lizards are small and can easily be injured with this method, it is not generally recommended.

Behavioral Differences

If in doubt about the sex of certain lizards, observing the behavior of animals often offers valuable clues. When in breeding condition, many male lizards perform territorial displays and aggressive, as well as reproductive, behaviors that make their sex unmistakable. Obviously, any lizard that lays eggs or gives birth is a female.

Veterinary Methods

Specialized veterinarians can perform other sexing methods, such as X-rays, caudal saline injections, and laparoscopy, on animals that cannot readily be sexed. It is hoped that the other methods discussed above will allow you to sex most insect-eating lizards without resorting to such procedures.

CHAPTER 5

QUARANTINE AND ACCLIMATION

I f you are purchasing a lizard for the first time and do not own animals other than the one you have just obtained, this section may not apply to you. However, if you think you will be buying other animals in the future, definitely read this section.

Even if you have purchased several lizards from the same enclosure in captivity, it is recommended that these lizards be quarantined and kept individually. However, many herpetoculturists keep animals from the same group together and quarantine them that way to save on space and labor.

After careful selection, quarantine and acclimation are two of the most important steps in the successful keeping of insect-eating lizards. It is important for any herpetoculturist

Keep newly acquired lizards in a quarantine setup, as shown.

to realize that if a lizard is not captive-bred and -raised (which applies to only a minority of those sold in the trade), it will have been wild-collected. This means it will also be infested with a number of parasites and is likely to have been exposed to a number of disease-causing organisms. Stressful conditions from transport, lack of food or water, and human interaction are common during an animal's initial period in captivity. As a result, parasites can increase to life-threatening levels, and the lizard may very well become much more susceptible to disease. It is critical that you always quarantine a newly acquired wild-caught lizard before introducing it into an established collection.

For most species, this means keeping a new lizard by itself in a quarantine enclosure isolated from other lizards in the collection, preferably in a separate room. The quarantine enclosure should be simply designed but provide the basic requirements of the animal, including a suitable substrate, basking areas and shelters, heat, and light. (With all but fossorial species, which need a substrate into which they can tunnel, newsprint is recommended as substrate during quarantine.) The minimum recommended quarantine period is thirty days; sixty to ninety days is preferable. During the quarantine period, you should daily spend varying amounts of time observing the animal and adjusting your maintenance schedules and procedures to meet its needs.

Quarantining your new pet will allow you to determine the following factors:

Whether an animal is feeding and drinking and whether it is maintaining or gaining weight: Close observation will also allow you to determine food preferences. For example, some of the small ant-eating agamas will initially feed on medium crickets in captivity, but they will invariably regurgitate them. If offered smaller crickets and fruit flies, the lizards will keep them down and gain weight.

The status of an animal's stools: Because of poor diet and other factors (including stress), it is common for newly imported animals to have soft stools. After a few days to a week, most animals should have the formed stools characteristic of a healthy lizard. Animals with per-

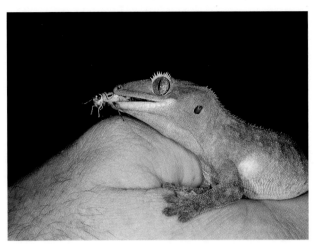

Observe new lizards to ensure that they are eating well and gaining weight.

sistently runny or discolored stools often have a gastroenteric disease that needs to be diagnosed and treated. The use of newsprint as a substrate allows you to easily assess the status of the stools.

The presence of parasites: External parasites (ticks and mites) can be observed and treated. Internal parasites are best determined by a fecal exam, but many herpetoculturists, particularly with smaller and inexpensive species, routinely treat their animals with fenbendazole (Panacur) at a dosage of 50 mg/kg (an accurate scale is required) for nematodes, and metronidazole (Flagyl) at a dosage of 50 mg/kg for protozoa. The treatment is repeated in ten to fifteen days. Some type of training is recommended before attempting home parasite treatment because there are overdose risks if you do not calculate accurately. (Two recommended references are Klingenberg [2007] and Mader [2006]). Another approach that is, in fact, used by most lizard keepers is to simply observe the animal. If it is feeding, maintaining good weight, and has healthy-appearing stools, it is presumed to be free of life-threatening levels of parasites.

Whether an animal is sick: Indications of illness are failure to feed, listlessness, weight loss, runny or discolored stools, swelling of limbs or lumps on the body, inability to move or to keep eyes open, sunken eyes, unusual (such as twitching of hind legs) or spasmodic behaviors, gaping,

Look out for external parasites, such as the red mites around the eye of this gecko.

and forced exhalation (almost always indicates respiratory infection or, on rare occasions, parasites). The sooner you determine a lizard to be ill and the sooner you attempt to determine what is wrong, the better the chances are that it will eventually pull through.

Necessary modifications in the vivarium design: Depending on a lizard's behavior in its enclosure, you may need to adjust the design. For example, if a newly purchased lizard consistently lies quietly at the end of the vivarium farthest from the heat source, the vivarium may be too warm. An alternate thermal gradient may need to be established. In another situation, an animal may always lie beneath or on a heat source, suggesting that the vivarium may not be warm enough.

Whether an animal is acclimating to captive conditions: The health of imported lizards often declines because of disease and environmental stress. This may begin subtly with gradual weight loss, but it can also take place quite suddenly, even overnight. The sooner you notice a decline and begin investigating its cause, the better the chances of the animal turning around. A lizard that is acclimating well will have the appearance of improved health, including weight gain, by the time the quarantine period is over.

CHAPTER 6

ESSENTIAL CONCEPTS

There are two essential concepts, or "big pictures," every herpetoculturist should keep in mind in the course of determining the best methods for raising and breeding lizards. One is ontogeny, which focuses on the requirements of developmental stages of a species. The other is a multifactorial model, which looks at how interacting factors such as temperature and diet contribute to the success of keeping animals long term.

Ontogeny for Herpetoculturists

We humans eventually learn that the requirements of babies or young children are different than those of adolescents, mature adults, or seniors. The notion of ontogeny, that an organism undergoes stages of development from embryo to old age, is naturally acquired as a consequence of experience and social interactions. Ontogeny is also an essential concept in herpetoculture, and it is important to keep in mind when developing methods for successfully keeping and breeding different species of lizards. Embryos in incubating eggs, for

The adult and newborn Jackson's chameleons shown here have very different needs.

41

example, are affected by different factors than hatchling lizards are, which in turn are affected by different factors than mature or older adults are.

For the purpose of herpetoculture, the ontogeny of lizards is best categorized as the following stages:

Embryonic

This stage begins following fertilization and ends with hatching. For most species of lizard, the embryonic stage is spent mostly outside of the mother's body within the confines of a shelled egg. With the few ovoviviparous and viviparous lizard species, this stage occurs within unshelled eggs or, in viviparous lizards, membranes within the mother's body.

The mother's nutrition and consequent yolk reserves, the lizards' genetics, substrate qualities including moisture, and incubation temperature can all have critical effects at this stage and will directly impact the survivability of embryos and the vigor of hatchlings. With some species of lizards, such as a number of geckos and anoles, temperature during the first two to three weeks of incubation will determine sex.

Hatchling lizards, such as these short-horned lizards (*Phrynosoma douglassi*) require special care.

Hatchling to Subadult

This stage begins with hatching and ends with sexual onset. With most species, it is characterized by rapid growth. Although many lizards are socially tolerant at this stage, some can demonstrate a significant degree of cannibalism or mutilation, usually exhibited by larger, more vigorous animals toward smaller ones, such as bearded dragons and gargoyle geckos. Because growth is rapid during this stage, keepers must take care to provide enough food and supplementation to prevent deficiencies and the risk of metabolic bone disease.

Sexual Onset and Peak Reproduction

This stage begins with the appearance of well-defined secondary sexual characteristics and the initial ability to reproduce. With the onset of this stage, some energy resources that were used for growth are diverted toward egg production and territorial, sociosexual behaviors. However, many lizard species first breed when they are less than half their mature adult size. Adjustments in diet and supplementation may be required at this stage (e.g., supplying extra calcium to gravid females). Sexual onset is the beginning of this stage, but it is followed by several years of peak breeding output. Growth rate continues to be significant during this period, with many of the larger lizards commonly growing to double or more their weight at sexual onset.

Maturity

There is a common misconception that reptiles grow throughout their lives, but experience shows that most species reach a growth wall beyond which little significant growth occurs. For example, a seven-year-old bearded dragon or leopard gecko is not significantly larger than a three-year-old. Thus, maturity is characterized by animals having reached near maximum size, with no significant growth.

An animal's mature size can be double its size or more at sexual onset. For many smaller species of lizards, it often takes the lizard twice the time to reach mature size as it did to reach sexual onset when raised under optimal husbandry conditions. Mature animals will have a few years with high reproductive rates, but for many, reproductive rates will eventually decline within a period about twice the amount of time it took to reach maturity.

Old Age

We have little information on the signs of old age in senior lizards. A common feature of aging in the females of many species is reduced to no reproductive output. For example, blue-tongue skinks and leopard geckos over about nine years old will often live for many years as nonbreeding adults. In some species, such as panther chameleons, males will show declining fertility by five years of age, with few copulations resulting in fertile or viable eggs. Eating less and failing to gain or maintain weight is common with older lizards. Shed problems such as skin adhering may also occur. Old age ends with death.

The Multifactorial Model of Herpetoculture

Although it's tempting to be simplistic when presenting ideas, life isn't always simple. Some of the most erroneous information perpetuated by the so-called reptile experts found on the Internet suffers from simplistic interpretations of husbandry factors. Successful husbandry methods are the

Proper husbandry, which includes adequate vivaria and appropriate food, will help keep your lizard healthy.

Parents pass on both good and bad health traits to their offspring.

result of many interacting factors, and within certain parameters, there can be more than one way to successfully maintain lizards. You may also find that the conditions that are optimal for reproductive output may not be the same conditions for a long-lived pet. The interacting factors that will determine success, whatever you deem success to be, fall under the following categories: genetics, ontogeny, climatic factors, landscape and environmental factors, diet and water, social factors, and disease.

Genetics
We know that good genetics are essential for vigor or survivability, but in herpetoculture, various morphs may have distinct requirements. One problem with captive-bred animals is that there is little culling and selection for vigor, so many individuals that are small or show diminished vigor are offered for sale. It is essential that breeders select for vigor to have long-term success.

Ontogeny
Developmental stages may have different requirements and tolerances. For example, the hatchlings of many species (e.g., most chameleons) are more difficult to maintain and raise than adults are.

Climatic Factors

Reptiles are endotherms; their body temperature depends on environmental temperatures. This is why providing the proper temperature range for a species is critical for its optimal health and survival. Although each species has an optimal temperature for feeding, growth, and activity, individuals have tolerances that will allow them to survive within a range outside that optimal temperature.

In captivity, we usually provide a warmer basking site and a cooler background temperature, which allows lizards to thermoregulate. However, suboptimal or too high temperatures are a common cause when lizards do not fare well in captivity. Two other climatic factors are relative humidity and ventilation. Although higher relative humidity tends to reduce loss of water by lizards, too high a relative humidity, combined with poor ventilation, can indirectly lead to fatal diseases, including bacterial and fungal infections. You can make up for water loss by providing regular water; however, a minimum relative humidity is required by many species for successful shedding.

Housing too many lizards together can lead to stress and anxiety among the occupants.

The factors that lead to long-term success at keeping and breeding lizards can be identified only through regular observation and careful record keeping. Although this practice is not always easy in today's busy world, records allow us to identify animals that may have health problems, that are genetically weak, or that do not meet our goals as herpetoculturists, including fecundity, size potential, or recessive traits.

The most common way to keep records is to label animals or their cages and maintain ID records that track specific individuals and, when possible, their ancestral background. Keeping good records makes it possible to identify the parentage of an outstanding hatchling so that more can be obtained in the future. If working with recessive traits, knowing the background of individuals is essential in order to breed the expression of that trait in its homozygous form.

Other common records maintained are regular measurements of size (total length or snout-to-vent length) and weight. For commercial purposes, lizard species that grow fast and large are generally preferable to slow-growing ones. Failure to gain or maintain weight is also a good indicator of a health problem, such as a parasite or bacterial infection. For breeders, the most important records are those that show breeding performance and fecundity. Breeders' records have allowed herpetoculturists to recognize that many lizards have a limited period or potential for high egg production or, in the case of males, for high fertility. Thus, larger and older lizards may not be the best choice for purchase when captive breeding is a primary goal. This is also why breeders schedule complete replacement of their breeding groups based on the fecundity data they have accumulated over time. There are many other types of records that can be kept (e.g., crest size and head width in crested geckos or differences in growth when lizards are fed different diets); these should be tailored to meet your particular goals.

Landscape Factors

Lizards have evolved adaptations to their particular niche. Chameleons and anoles require branches for climbing. Many skinks need a burrowing medium to fare well. Most terrestrial lizards will seek shelter for part of the day and to sleep in at night. Landscaping creates microenvironments with specific temperature and humidity levels that are essential for the welfare of many lizard species.

Diet and Water

A properly balanced diet is critical for the long-term survival of lizards. However, lizards, like humans, will grow and survive on less than optimal diets as long as certain minimum requirements are met. In captivity, commercial insects are a staple diet of many lizards, but the insects must be supplemented or properly gut loaded to provide the required calcium and vitamins. A UV source will help determine how much vitamin D_3 supplementation is required. Diets that may be suitable for optimal growth in juveniles may not be ideal for adults.

Lizards obtain their water from food or by drinking. Most lizards will drink from shallow water containers, but many arboreal species drink from droplets from falling rain or dew, so they require misting or dripping instead of a drinking bowl.

Social Factors

Social stress from overcrowding or bullying by a dominant animal can limit access to food or reduce an affected animal's appetite, leading to a reduced growth rate. Anorexia, combined with the side effects of stress such as depression of the immune system, can lead to illness and death. Aggression between members of the same species can lead to injuries. With many lizard species, multiple males cannot be kept in the same enclosure; with others, both sexes may be territorial and aggressive.

Disease

The ability of a reptile to fight disease depends in part on temperature. Optimal temperatures allow lizards to digest and metabolize efficiently. Optimal temperatures also optimize the efficiency of the immune system. Relative humidity is another environmental factor that significantly affects lizards' health. When relative humidity is too low, it can lead to shedding problems and high rates of water loss. When it is too high, especially in poorly ventilated enclosures, it can lead to bacterial and fungal infections. An inadequate diet is another common cause of illness in lizards.

Relative Surface-to-Volume Ratios

An important principle in herpetoculture is that of relative surface-to-volume ratios. Briefly, this principle states that all other things being equal (e.g., same species and body proportions), the larger an object or animal, the smaller its relative surface-to-volume ratio. Conversely, the smaller an object or animal, the greater its relative surface-to-volume ratio. To make this more understandable, let us take as an example the relative surface-to-volume ratios of two cubes. One cube has 1-foot sides and the other has 2-foot sides.

The surface of one side (a) of a cube is side x side (a x a = a^2). To obtain the total surface, you multiply the surface of one side (a^2) by the number of sides (6). The volume of a cube is side x side x side (a x a x a = a^3).

In the case of cube A:
Surface of one side is 1 ft. x 1 ft = 1 sq ft
Total surface is 1 sq ft x 6 = 6 sq ft
Volume is 1 x 1 x 1 = 1 cu ft
Surface-to-volume ratio is 6 to 1

In the case of cube B:
Surface of one side is 2 ft. x 2 ft = 4 sq ft
Total surface is 4 sq ft x 6 = 24 sq ft
Volume is 2 x 2 x 2 = 8 cu ft
Surface-to-volume ratio is 3 to 1

In terms of herpetoculture, this is important because smaller animals have a greater surface-to-volume ratio. Thus, they heat up and cool down faster than large animals do. They can usually digest their food faster as well. Their rate of metabolism is higher, partially because the surface-to-volume ratio applies internally as well as externally. Small animals dehydrate faster than larger animals do. As a rule, disease will tend to overtake smaller reptiles in less time than it will larger reptiles.

The same principle applies to crickets. Small crickets have a higher surface-to-volume ratio than large crickets do. When coating small crickets, the amount of vitamin-mineral supplement can be proportionately two or more times the amount adhering to large crickets. This can be beneficial in some cases, but in others it can lead to hypervitaminosis, such as hypervitaminosis A (which is proving to be a significant problem with some species).

This principle can also be applied to vivarium design. Stratifying space in a vivarium essentially subdivides a large volume into a number of smaller ones and thereby increases the available surface area.

In addition to environmental factors, other disease factors include parasitism and a range of bacterial, protozoan, fungal, or viral infections. Many of these diseases are transmitted by other infected animals, but others are a consequence of inadequate environmental conditions.

Addressing these factors will contribute to the health and longevity of the lizard(s) you keep. Within constraint parameters, the interacting factors can vary and still lead to success.

CHAPTER 7

TYPES OF VIVARIA

From the point of view of lizard keeping, there are four main types of vivaria: desert, forest floor, tropical forest, and shoreline. These are arbitrary groupings created by herpetoculturists that do not necessarily correspond to the established use of the terms or to biomes/life zones (e.g., a desert vivarium is not exclusively for desert-dwelling lizards).

Desert Vivaria

This type of vivarium is characterized by a dry substrate of either sand or fine gravel. It has one or more hot basking areas created by spotlights plus one or more shelters. A hot rock–type heater can be used as a secondary heating source. Rocks and dry woods are used to landscape and create basking areas, shelters, and humidity zones. You can also incorporate some live plants, such as sansevierias, ponytail palms, haworthias, and others.

Desert vivaria generally have sand or fine gravel substrates.

Daytime temperatures should be in the low to mid-80s F (28.9°C to 30°C), with basking areas from 87°F to 100°F (30.6°C to 37.8°C). This type of vivarium also includes a marked drop in nighttime temperatures, usually down to room temperature, or 70s F (21°C to 26°C) during the warm months. Lizards from dry montane areas typically require a greater drop in nighttime temperatures. Relative humidity is typically low to moderate because of the low moisture content of the substrate and high evaporative rate generated by spotlights in desert vivaria. Winter temperatures should be determined by the requirements of the particular species. To prevent too much humidity, provide water only in a shallow dish; water plants individually at the base.

Lizards that do well in desert vivaria include desert agamines, including several *Agama* species; bearded dragons (*Pogona*); many skinks, such as Schneider's skinks and barrel skinks (*Chalcides*); plated lizards; girdle-tailed lizards (armadillo lizards of the pet trade); lacertids; and geckos from dry, desert, and semi-arid areas. If using a fine sand substrate, use desert vivaria for desert and semi-arid region fossorial species, such as sandfish and ocellated skinks. If the relative humidity is moderate, desert vivaria can be used with many tropical dry forest species.

Some herpetoculturists combine features of a forest floor vivarium and a tropical forest vivarium in one enclosure so that they can keep a variety of species together. However, large vivaria are required in order to accomplish this.

Forest Floor, Moist Substrate Vivaria

This type of vivarium requires a barely moist substrate, usually composed of a flaky, airy moist potting soil mix or a damp mulch, such as cypress mulch. Some herpetoculturists use seeding orchid bark. The substrate should have sufficient depth for the upper surface to remain dry. The substrate will depend on the species kept in the vivarium; some species need a sandier substrate, whereas sand is too abrasive for other species.

A few rocks or a dried tree stump or root base can be used for landscaping, as can several species of live plants such as pothos, sansevieria, and smaller philodendrons. Lizards will use these for climbing, basking, and hiding. Several shelters should be included to provide the animal a place to hide and to increase relative humidity. Relative humidity builds up within the shelters as a result of trapping water evaporation from the substrate.

Tropical forest vivaria require branches for climbing and plants for hiding.

53

Heating depends on the species kept in the vivarium. For tropical species, a subtank heater will maintain an even ground temperature. For montane or temperate species, no subtank heat is required. Place a spotlight over a basking area (rock or tree stump) so that basking temperatures are in the mid-80s F (28.9°C to 30°C).

The lizards recommended for a forest floor, moist substrate vivarium include burrowing forest skinks such as several of the small Asian *Mabuya*; *Lygosoma*; various anguids, such as the European slow worm (*Anguis fragilis*); and some of the galliwasps.

Tropical Forest and Arboreal Lizard Vivaria

This type of vivarium is usually used by arboreal or semi-arboreal tropical forest lizards. It is characterized by a dry substrate surface, typically orchid bark or a moist soil mix, with a dry upper surface. Place a basking light over a dried tree stump or over a diagonally placed branch for arboreal and semi-arboreal species. A subtank heater, such as Flexwatt, should be used to help maintain the vivarium at an evenly warm temperature in the mid-80s F (28.9°C to 30°C) during the day, with a 5 to 10 degrees drop at night. Dried woods and live plants can be used for landscaping. Good plants are pothos,

Chinese evergreen, dracaenas, *Sansevieria trifasciata* and hybrids, bromeliads such as neoregelias and earth stars (*Cryptanthus*), and many others. Relative humidity should be moderate to high, depending on the substrate moisture, plants, and misting regimens. Watering for arboreal species is provided primarily by misting, but it is a good idea to also place a small, shallow water container in the enclosure.

Arboreal lizards, such as chameleons, anoles, basilisks, arboreal agamines, water dragons, day geckos, and many other climbing geckos, do well in tropical forest vivaria.

Shoreline Vivaria

This type of vivarium combines land and water. Because the only semi-aquatic lizard species available in the pet trade at present are the water skinks (*Tropidophorus*), the basic design for this vivarium is simple. Crocodile lizards (*Shinisaurus crocodilurus*) can also be kept in shoreline vivaria but must be in enclosures at least 36 inches long.

A shoreline vivarium requires at least 24 inches (60.9 cm) in length. Aquarium gravel is used to create a ground level that slopes into a water section. Rocks are placed at the edge of the water. Freshwater driftwood can also be added to the vivarium. Plants such as pothos, arrowheads (*Syngonium*), and Chinese evergreen (*Aglaonema*) are grown hydroponically. A subtank heater on a thermostat maintains the overall tank temperature in the high 70s F (25°C to 26°C), and a basking light is placed over the rocks so that temperature is in the mid-80s F (28.9°C to 30°C) (use a small spotlight). The vivarium can be flushed by pouring water through the gravel and then siphoning it out through the water section.

Note: In a well-designed vivarium, water skinks make an attractive and interesting display. They will breed in captivity; they give birth to live young.

Temperate and Montane Lizards

The temperatures, substrates, and plant selections used in the above-described vivarium types can also be adjusted to meet the requirements of various temperate and montane lizard species.

CHAPTER 8

ENCLOSURES

A variety of enclosures ranging from plastic or glass terrariums to screen cages are now offered for different reptile species. Each has its value depending on the purpose (temporary or long-term housing, quarantine, juvenile rearing) and the species selected for.

All-Glass Vivaria

My preferred vivaria are front-opening, all-glass enclosures because they make a nice display, offer good visibility, and are scratch resistant. These can be found in specialized reptile stores and can be purchased from mail-order suppliers on the Internet. Not as ideal, but more readily available, are all-glass enclosures with sliding screen tops. You can also use an aquarium tank, as long as a secure-fitting screen top is bought or constructed and added to the enclosure. For geckos that climb on glass, enclosures with side openings, which are available by special order, are recommended to prevent sudden escapes through the top.

There are a variety of enclosures that can work for lizards, both commercially available and homemade.

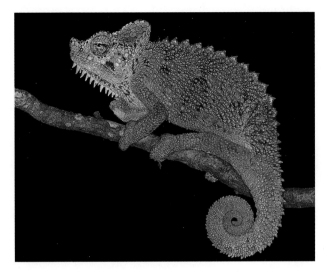

Most chameleons, such as this *Chamaeleo (trioceros) hoehnelii,* fare best in screen cages.

Custom-Built Enclosures

If you live near an all-glass vivarium manufacturer, you may consider having a vivarium custom built. Commercially sold all-glass vivaria usually do not have sufficient room for creating interesting stratification. For example, placing a background of rock or cork bark in a commercial tank usually takes up so much of the available space that the amount of remaining open space is significantly affected. A commercial manufacturer, which can be found through magazines or on the Internet, may be willing to build a custom aquarium with larger dimensions. Custom-made enclosures constructed of wood or melamine with sliding glass doors in front are also available from individuals and small companies specializing in reptile enclosures. These are suitable only for animals that can be kept on a dry substrate.

You can also construct a larger enclosure yourself using a wood bottom and sides, glass front, and a screened cover. If you use wood, apply several coats of marine epoxy paint or clear polyurethane to seal the wood against moisture (be sure the product you choose is safe for the animals). You can build very large custom enclosures using aluminum-frame windows, fiberglass tub enclosures, or shower stalls with clear glass doors.

Do not use acrylic aquarium tanks or Plexiglas-sided enclosures to house lizards. The animals scratch the sides to the point that the aesthetic appeal of the enclosure is eventually lost.

Open-Top Vivaria

Open-top vivaria can be used with terrestrial lizards, particularly species from desert or semi-arid habitats. Custom-made enclosures of wood, melamine, preformed large plastic tubs or troughs, and fiberglass enclosures, including small hot tubs, are suitable for this type of setup. Interesting naturalistic landscapes can be designed with open-top vivaria. Make the bottom of the enclosure waterproof by inserting a custom Plexiglas liner, a polyethylene liner (sold in rolls in hardware stores), or a pool liner (obtainable from stores or nurseries offering materials for water gardens).

Because this type of vivarium is more easily accessible than others, it's not recommended for homes with young children, cats, or dogs. To minimize the risk of escapes, create a lip around the inside of the upper edge. To ensure that an animal that accidentally escapes remains within a limited area, open-top vivaria should always be kept in a secure room, with no space under the door and all small holes in the walls or floor sealed.

Wire Mesh- and Screen-Sided Vivaria

Plastic-coated, welded wire mesh cages and aviaries are suitable for large chameleons and some large arboreal lizards (plain wire mesh, however, is not appropriate). Screen-sided vivaria made of aluminum or plastic screen are suitable for keeping chameleons, anoles, and small lizards, as long as attention is given to providing proper relative humidity. However, these vivaria are seldom visually attractive and have considerable limitations in terms of design and landscaping potential.

Plastic Storage Boxes

Plastic storage boxes (such as Rubbermaid) are useful for large-scale maintenance of nocturnal terrestrial geckos. Small

You can make your own custom screen enclosure. This one is ideal for chameleons.

perforations must be placed in the top and sides for air flow. They have proven to be economical and space-saving enclosures. They can be kept on shelves heated with recessed heat tape or narrow Flexwatt heat strips, which run the length of the shelf underneath the boxes and are controlled by thermostat or rheostat. Plastic storage boxes can be used for large-scale maintenance of small diurnal lizards as long as a custom screen cover is built and a light source is placed above. Several gecko breeders also prefer a screen top with light over a perforated top.

Plastic Terraria

Commercially sold plastic terraria are not generally recommended for keeping insect-eating lizards. They are adequate for some very small species of lizards, but for the most part, their use is limited. In most cases, plastic terraria are too small. In addition, the plastic can melt when exposed to heat sources. The plastic also eventually becomes scratched, resulting in limiting the viewing of the terrarium's occupants.

Breeders often use plastic cages for keeping a large number of reptiles.

Plastic terraria are, however, useful for raising and segregating baby lizards, as long as they are kept in heated rooms and the only heat source is fluorescent full-spectrum lighting or thermostatically controlled thin heat tape. Breeders of geckos and true chameleons find plastic terraria very useful during the early stages of rearing these lizards. They are also practical for transporting smaller lizards and for housing insects while they are being gut loaded.

Outdoor Vivaria

In areas where the climate is moderate, insect-eating lizards can be kept in outdoor vivaria for part of the year or even year-round. Specially designed greenhouses, screen houses, and custom-built outdoor vivaria are suitable for this purpose.

Because outdoor vivaria must create generally the same conditions as indoor vivaria, careful thought must be given to their design. For example, the sun can provide light and heat, and water can be supplied through automated misters or drip systems. During the winter months, heat must be provided through a heating system, otherwise the animals will need to be brought indoors. It is not within the scope of this book to provide details on the design of outdoor vivaria.

Size of Enclosures

In terms of enclosure size, a vivarium should be at least four times as long as the total length of the largest lizard, and the width should be at least one and a half times the length of the largest lizard. A naturalistic vivarium containing plants and elaborate landscaping should be at least five times the length of the largest lizard. I prefer larger vivaria—at least eight times the length of the largest lizard for small species and at least four times the length of the largest lizard for medium to large species. Taller vivaria are recommended for use with arboreal or semi-arboreal species. It is important to think in terms of the reptiles' quality of life, just as you would with other kinds of animals.

If you are keeping more than one lizard in an enclosure, keep in mind that reptiles fare best when they are not over-crowded. The sum of the total lengths of the lizards in one enclosure should be less than three-quarters the length of the enclosure. If you are mixing two species of lizards that inhabit different niches, such as small lacertas (e.g., *Podarcis muralis*), which are ground- and rock-dwelling, with crocodile geckos

Some keepers who are lucky enough to live in temperate climates keep their lizards outdoors all or part of the year.

For very large animals, you may need a walk-in type of lizard cage.

(*Tarentola mauritanica*), which are rock- and bark-climbing (also side-dwellers in vivaria), then the density can be slightly increased. Remember: lower density leads to lower stress levels, a lower of risk of spreading disease, and less maintenance. The criteria for animal density are often the same as for effective breeding groups: single pairs or trios (one male with two females) of a given species.

Mixing Species

As a rule, it is best to not mix lizard species, particularly if you are interested in captive breeding. If you are working with rare species or are serious about captive breeding, do not mix species.

Many herpetoculturists have had good results mixing species as long as they mix species that do not compete for the same vivarium niche. For example, some people successfully keep together several species of Egyptian lizards, including fossorial species such as ocellated skinks (*Chalcides ocellatus*), diurnal ground-dwelling species such as lacertas, and rock- or wall-dwelling species such as fan-footed geckos (*Ptyodactylus hasselquistii*) or Moorish geckos (*Tarentola mauritanica*). Here, again, experimentation is required.

CHAPTER 9

VIVARIUM DESIGN

O nce you decide on the species you want to keep, it is time to design and landscape your future pet's vivarium. This will require some investigation and planning to create a display that best suits your lizard's needs.

Steps to Vivarium Design

The following steps are required to assemble a vivarium:

1. Select an enclosure.
2. Place enclosure on a stand or other item of furniture.
3. If a subtank heating system is used, place the heater under the enclosure.
4. Place the substrate(s) in the bottom of the enclosure.
5. Add landscape structures, including shelters, basking areas, rocks, and wood.
6. Add plants and possibly add more surface layer substrate.
7. Place the cover over the top.

This vivarium has everything its occupant requires, including a hide box and an undertank heat plate.

8. Add lights and other heating systems.

9. Add monitoring equipment such as timers, thermometers, and hygrometers.

10. Make adjustments as required.

Substrates

For many species of desert lizards, various sands, gravels, and sand-soil mixes make suitable substrates. For desert species that dig burrows, use a substrate consisting of 50 percent sand and 50 percent potting soil, or a sandy soil containing clay, at one end of the enclosure. Moisten that section, and then pat down the soil to compress it. When it dries, the compressed soil usually retains the necessary cohesion to allow for digging a burrow. If you live near a desert, consider using natural desert soils. The rest of the vivarium can contain sand. Some vivarists search for the larger-grained sand and soils found at the entrances of nests of certain large ants because they have a natural appearance and are neither too fine nor too coarse. Just be sure not to collect any ants at the same time. When available, decomposed granite sands are excellent for desert vivaria.

For forest and arboreal species, you can use a fine- to medium-grade orchid bark (use a grade large enough so that it cannot be readily swallowed), which is attractive and retains

The substrate you use will depend on the species you intend to keep. Desert species generally require a sand or sandlike substrate.

Ant Control

Ants can be the nemesis of lizard keepers. These insects are usually unintentionally introduced into a vivarium with live plants. They can trail and swarm to feed on dead food insects and fruit nectars. They may try to set up a colony within the vivarium. Sometimes they will even swarm and kill baby lizards.

Inspect plants very carefully before introducing them into a vivarium. Also, be sure to control ant populations in and around your home. With some more sensitive lizard species, such as day geckos and true chameleons, you may need to protect babies from ants by raising them in watertight enclosures sitting in shallow containers of water. Some chameleon keepers put the legs of custom-built enclosure stands in containers filled with motor oil or water to keep ants out. Beware: It is much easier to guard against ants beforehand than it is to deal with them after you have established a vivarium.

some moisture when dampened. A good-quality moistened potting soil (without perlite) can also be used effectively with these species. The surface of the potting soil should be allowed to dry, or top the potting soil with a thin layer of dry substrate, such as orchid bark. For naturalistic vivaria containing small forest or arboreal species, use a substrate consisting of a peat-base potting soil with 10 to 20 percent medium-grade sand and 10 to 20 percent fine orchid bark placed over a 1½ inch (3.8 cm) layer of pebbles. This combination of soil, sand, bark, and a layer of pebbles will increase drainage. An orchid bark substrate presents problems with small species because food items (small crickets) are able to hide all too easily.

Landscaping

How you landscape your vivarium depends on the needs and behaviors of its inhabitants. Arboreal and climbing lizards should be provided with dried branches and sections of wood or cork bark slabs for climbing. Rock-climbing species from desert areas should have vertical sections of cholla wood, dried wood sections, or cork bark. You can also construct climbing areas using rocks, but take great care to

Avoid Silica Sand

Fine silica sand is not recommended for active digging species because of a possible risk of silicosis of the lungs. Also, silica sand may abrade and scar the GI tract of baby lizards if it is ingested.

assure that the rocks cannot shift or fall, accidentally crushing the lizards. Silicone cement will hold rocks together and help prevent these mishaps. Hot glue also works with some kinds of rock. Generally, lighter substitutes, such as sand-blasted woods, cholla skeleton, and cork make maintenance easier (you won't ever have to lift heavy rocks) and are safer for the animals. There are also plastic landscape materials simulating rocks and wood that are suitable. Molded fiberglass backgrounds copied directly from rocky areas are an alternative that will be available in the near future.

Shelters
Except for arboreal species that sleep on branches, all lizards should be provided with some kind of shelter.

Vertical Shelters
Climbing lizards, such as geckos, require vertical shelters. These are easily created by placing slabs of cork bark or rock vertically against the side of the enclosure. Take care to anchor rocks well to prevent crushing.

Horizontal Shelters
Terrestrial lizards require horizontal shelters. These are shelters that are placed over the substrate of the vivarium. There are several attractive, commercially produced shelters of formed concrete, plastic, ceramic, and clay that work well. Cork bark is another excellent choice for horizontal shelters. Shelters can also be made from broken sections of clay pots or by resting one thin rock over another. When using rocks, take care not to accidentally crush lizards when removing or moving the rocks. Silicone sealant or hot glue can hold rocks together and help to reduce that risk.

Aboveground Shelters

Some arboreal lizards, such as prehensile-tailed geckos (*Rhacodactylus*) and a number of rock-dwelling lizards, prefer aboveground shelters. These shelters should be placed on a horizontal platform or shelf that is adhered to the side of the vivarium using silicone sealant. The platform can be made of glass sections, cork bark, or wood. You can also adhere the cork bark or wood to each other to form stacks. Rock platforms can also be adhered to the walls of the vivarium, but beware of the risk of lizards being crushed and of glass breaking. Access to these aboveground shelters can be created by using sections of cork, wood, or rock.

Humidified Shelters

One of the features of shelters and burrows in the wild, particularly in drier habitats, is that the relative humidity inside a shelter is significantly higher than in the open air. The result is that reptiles in shelters lose less water while breathing. The higher relative humidity also facilitates shedding. Humidified shelters have been used with a variety of reptiles. They have proven particularly useful with certain desert geckos, such as frog-eyed geckos (*Teratoscincus*), fat-tail geckos (*Hemitheconyx*

You can use common household items to supply a hide box for your lizard.

caudicinctus), and the Australian eyelash geckos (*Diplodactylus*). Humidified shelters also reduce life-threatening water loss when acclimating certain species.

The following are three approaches to creating humidified shelters:

1. Place a small shallow dish of sand, pebbles, or a mix of both in the center of an oversize shelter. The substrate-filled dish is then sprayed regularly so that the contents stay moist. Lizards can choose the dry or the moist substrate as they prefer.

2. Shelters made of red kiln-baked clay have water-holding qualities that contribute to relative humidity. Simply place the shelter in water for about an hour; then place it in the vivarium. As the water evaporates, humidity is increased. Soak the shelter every one to three days.

Many lizards require basking lamps.

3. Place a small, nontippable water container in the shelter. For example, an empty film canister can be attached to the side of a shelter using silicone sealer. The canister can then be filled with water. As the water evaporates, it raises the relative humidity.

Basking Areas

To fare well, most diurnal lizards require a basking area, over which a high temperature is generated. A basking area helps establish a gradient whereby the temperature diminishes with distance from the heat source.

For terrestrial lizards, create a basking area by placing an incandescent light (either a regular household lightbulb or a spotlight) in a reflector-type fixture above the screen top of a vivarium so that heat is radiated onto a flat rock. For arboreal lizards, place branches or interesting sections of wood or tree root diagonally along the length of the vivarium as climbing areas. Place an incandescent light above the screen of the vivarium so that heat is radiated from the upper to the middle portion of the angled wood section, allowing lizards to thermoregulate depending on their distance from the heat source. When keeping several lizards together, provide two or more basking sites. Dominant animals may bully submissive individuals away from the site if there is only one.

Hot rock–type heaters and reptile heating pads are useful with some terrestrial and nocturnal species, but for most diurnal terrestrial species, they are recommended only as secondary heat sources. Many lizards associate basking with light. Hot rocks should not be used as a substitute for meeting the lighting requirements of lizards.

CHAPTER 10
NATURALISTIC VIVARIUM DESIGN

The term *naturalistic vivaria* refers to vivaria in which some of the essential elements of an animal's habitat are simulated by using live plants and a variety of landscape materials. The goal is to create an environment that allows the animals to fare well and display a wide range of behaviors, as well as being aesthetically appealing, even with no animals present. Although naturalistic vivarium design may be rare in the United States, it is part of mainstream European herpetoculture.

One key to naturalistic vivarium design is that you don't need to actually reproduce an animal's natural habitat because the native plants and landscape materials are rarely available. In addition, plants from the natural habitat seldom fare well

Although naturalistic vivaria can't exactly replicate a lizard's natural environment, they can provide some of the same conditions.

Live plants add to the beauty and function of a vivarium.

over time inside a vivarium. Instead, you select plants that are known to grow well in vivaria. For landscape materials, you may choose cork bark, lightweight fiberglass reproductions of rock or wood, or rocks made of formed concrete in place of natural rock. Artistic latitude is one of the privileges afforded in naturalistic vivarium design.

Low animal density is another important factor in successful vivarium design. This minimizes maintenance and damage to the display.

Plants

Plants add considerable appeal to a vivarium that houses insect-eating lizards. You can place plants in pots and bury the pots in the substrate or conceal them with landscape structures. Or, if you're keeping small lizards, place plants directly in the ground medium. Certain plants can be placed in jars of water and grown hydroponically.

The selection of plants for vivaria requires special consideration. Amphibians and reptiles are active animals, capable of crushing, tearing, and uprooting many commonly sold houseplants and terrarium plants. I have experimented with a wide range of plants in vivarium design and have created many successful naturalistic vivaria. Although it is not within the scope of this book to list all plant species suitable for

Artificial plants work well for larger lizards that may be too hard on live plants.

vivaria, the following plants species are relatively easy to obtain and fare well under the conditions indicated.

Desert Vivaria Plants

Here are plants that do well in desert vivaria:

Caudexed figs (*Ficus palmeri* and *Ficus petiolaris*)
Climbing aloe (*Aloe ciliaris*)
Gasteraloes
Gasterhaworthia 'Royal Highness'
Geranium species (*Pelargonium*)
Haworthias
Lace aloe (*Aloe aristata*)
Oxtongue or bowtie plants (*Gasteria*)
Partridge breast aloe (*Aloe variegata*)
Ponytail palms (*Beaucarnea recurvata*)
Snake plants (*Sansevieria*) (these make some of the best vivarium plants)

Note: Some cacti with no spines or with harmlessly recurved spines can be tried, but the risk of etiolation (lack of sun or enough light, resulting in deformed and elongated growth) is high. For this reason, I have not listed cacti here.

Tropical Vivaria Plants

These plants do well in tropical vivaria:

Bromeliads (*Neoregelia, Billbergia, Guzmania, Aechmea*) (species with spiny edges can present problems for large lizard species)

Chinese evergreen (*Aglaonema*)

Creeping fig (*Ficus pumila*)

Dracaenas (in small sizes; they eventually outgrow a vivarium)

Dwarf schefflera (*Brassaia actinophylla*)

Earth stars (*Cryptanthus*)

Orchids (*Dendrobium, Epidendrum, Haemaria, Oncidium,* and many others)

Pothos (*Epipremnum aureum*)

Rosary vine *(Ceropegia woodii)*

Snake plants (*Sansevieria*) (there are many species and quite variable)

Various Gesneriads, particularly *Nematanthus* and *Aeschynanthus*

Weeping fig (*Ficus benjamina)*

Sources of Plants

Plants suitable for vivaria can be found in supermarkets, department stores, plant shops, and nurseries. For those who live in isolated areas or who want unusual species not normally sold in stores, the best way to obtain interesting vivarium plants is through mail order. Check house plant publications for sources.

CHAPTER 11

HEATING

Most lizards require heat to fare well in captivity. Lizards generally require a temperature gradient in a vivarium, whereby the temperature is higher under a heated basking area and progressively cooler as the distance from the heat source increases. Failure to provide adequate heat leads to the lizards's refusal to feed, inactivity, and increasing susceptibility to disease. There are several systems for heating lizard enclosures currently available in herpetoculture. Unfortunately, little information is available on the proper use and respective limitations of these various systems. The following information should allow you to make wise choices in your selection of heating systems.

General Heating Principles

At the crux of the thinking about heating for reptile vivaria is the concept of the heat gradient: a range of temperatures and temperature-associated landscaping that reptiles can select from to maintain their optimal body temperature.

Before setting up a vivarium for lizards, consider how you are going to generate and control the ground temperature and background air temperature of the vivarium. With large collections, herpetoculturists often choose to heat the entire room to a level that will be suitable for most of the lizards, using either a central heating system or individual room or space heaters.

In most cases, the room temperature will be too cool as a background temperature on a year-round basis, so you will want to set up a heating system to maintain control of the vivarium temperature. As a general rule, heat from incandescent bulbs in reflectors will be the primary daytime heat source; these bulbs are placed over basking sites. For maintaining and controlling a suitable background temperature, reptile heat strips or heat pads (either with rheostats or on thermostats) can be installed underneath the vivaria. For nocturnal and burrowing species, reptile heating pads and strips can be used for maintaining a background temperature, and red lights, ceramic infrared bulbs, or temperature-controlled hot rocks are used for generating the high-heat sites.

Take great care when installing heating systems. There is always a risk of fire and electrocution when dealing with electrical heat-generating elements. Proceed carefully, and follow the manufacturers' instructions and notes of caution.

Incandescent Lighting (Tungsten Filament Bulbs)

The preferred method of providing a heat source for diurnal lizards is the use of incandescent bulbs (either regular bulbs or spotlights) in a proper fixture, usually with an aluminum reflector with holes near the base to allow for heat dissipation. These lights are typically placed above a screen cover. Some herpetoculturists place them on special stands, such

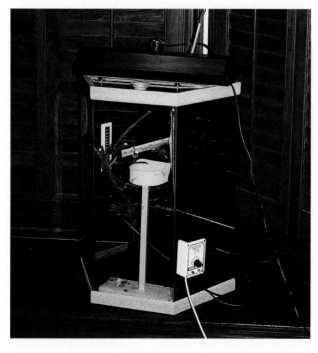

This vivarium provides adequate heating, humidity, and ventilation for its occupants.

A basking lamp provides heat and light.

A basking lamp provides heat and light.

as camera tripods (used with open vivaria). They are also sometimes used inside enclosures, with the bulb encased in a metal wire cage to protect the lizards from being burned.

Basking lights are generally suitable for a large number of terrestrial, arboreal, and some fossorial lizards that bask. For some nocturnal lizards, such as climbing geckos, low-wattage red incandescent bulbs can be a good heat source. However, with most nocturnal terrestrial species, alternative heat sources such as reptile heat pads or heat tape are preferred.

Be sure the fixture can handle the wattage and type of bulb you are using, or you could have a risk of fire. As with an incubator, the daytime temperature of a vivarium should be calibrated with the aid of a thermometer (preferably digital). By varying the wattage and type of incandescent bulbs used, you can achieve suitable temperature gradients within a vivarium. To do this, place the fixture in position over the basking area. Then place the thermometer on the basking area at the location closest to the fixture. Twenty to thirty minutes later, take a temperature reading. If the desired basking temperature is achieved, place the thermometer at the area in the vivarium farthest from the heat source. Wait ten minutes and take another reading (this will give the vivarium low temperature). If the temperature of the basking area is too high or too low, you can adjust it by using a lower or higher wattage bulb. The wattage of the bulbs may have to be changed to compensate for seasonal changes in temperature, that is, higher wattage in the winter and lower in the summer.

A light dimmer can be used to achieve the desired temperatures. There is also a proportional pulse-controlled thermostat on the market that works very well for this purpose, effectively eliminating concern about changing bulb wattage if the ambient room temperature changes. Vivarium design also affects the temperature gradient. A large vivarium allows for a wide range of available temperatures, whereas a small one, because of its limited surface area, allows for virtually no range. Remember: the lowest possible temperature in a vivarium is roughly equivalent to the ambient room temperature at the same height as the vivarium. As a rule, only low-wattage bulbs (25- to 60-watt regular bulbs or 50-watt spotlights) should be used with 10-gallon (37.9-liter) vivaria. The use of incandescent light fixtures with standard light bulbs or spotlights as a source of heat is generally not recommended with vivaria smaller than 10 gallons (37.9 liters) because providing a gradient becomes virtually impossible. Many lizards die from overheating as a result of the misuse of incandescent lighting.

There is a risk of overheating if the wrong wattage bulb is used. These bulbs are unsuitable for heating very small vivaria because all areas are exposed to the light, resulting in a lack of thermal gradient. There is a risk of overheating in small or partially covered vivaria as well as a risk of fire if the bulbs are placed near flammable materials. They can be expensive if used as the only heat source for a large collection.

Do not use incandescent bulbs as a primary heat source for smaller vivaria (24 inches [60.9 cm] or less) with covers that are part glass and part screen unless you carefully adjust the bulb wattage using a thermometer. The glass portion of the cover acts as a heat trap. Unless the vivarium is very large, this can result in the elimination of a thermal gradient, and life-threatening heat could build up. Partially covering the screen top of a vivarium with any solid material may have similar results.

Ceramic Infrared Heat Emitters

These emitters/bulbs produce a nice even heat without generating significant light, making them practical for use during both day and night. They are expensive yet long lived and prove particularly useful for heating vivaria at night in areas where rooms get too cold.

Care must be given when selecting a wattage (at this time 60-watt, 100-watt, and 150-watt emitters are available), or you could risk cooking your animal(s). Even the 60-watt emitter is best used with a vivarium at least 24 inches (60.9 cm) long. These emitters should be used in ceramic fixtures or fixtures capable of handling spotlights, ideally reflectors with holes near the base to allow for heat dissipation. Heat buildup in the reflector can shorten the life of the emitter and damage the fixture.

A thermometer is required with these bulbs, and a thermostat is highly recommended. During the day, this emitter should be used in conjunction with fluorescent light. Arrange the ceramic emitter so that the animal(s) cannot make direct contact with it. Place it over a basking areas located away from plants and landscape structures so they do not get baked. Rheostats and pulse-proportional thermostats can be used in conjunction with these emitters to adjust temperature.

There is a risk of overheating if the proper wattage emitter is not selected and if a thermometer or thermostat is not used. The fact that these emitters do not generate light when they are on can lead to accidental burn injuries of keepers.

Hot Rock–Type Heaters

Hot rocks provide localized heat that does not warm the air in a vivarium efficiently. They are best considered as a secondary heat source for terrestrial reptiles. Also, hot rocks do not create heat gradients, often creating a relatively cool vivarium temperature with a high hot rock temperature. In badly designed pet store setups, lizards sometimes congregate on the only warmth available, the hot rock.

These are best used for terrestrial geckos at night and as secondary heat sources for terrestrial lizards in conjunction with primary heat sources such as incandescent bulbs in reflectors. Always use hot rocks in conjunction with a thermometer to determine surface temperature. Units with built-in thermostats are preferable to those without.

There are problems with using hot rock–type heaters. If used in a vivarium that is otherwise inadequately heated, hot rocks encourage lizards to frequently bask on the hot rock because the rest of the vivarium is too cool. This limits activity and can lead to prolonged ventral heating that may be too high in the long term. Lizards may lie on their bellies against hot rocks for hours at a time. If the hot rock surface is too warm, subtle thermal burns or damage to belly scales can result. Even without surface burns, this type of long-term heat exposure may affect the internal organs and fertility of certain lizards, although this possibility has yet to be investigated.

At one time, the use of hot rocks meant that lizards had a choice of resting on 105°F (40.6°C) surfaces or being exposed to cold. Several manufacturers now offer hot rock–type heaters that operate within a safe heat range: 80s F (26.6°C to 31.7°C) for some; 90s F (32.2°C to 37.2°C) for others. More expensive versions of hot rock–type heaters, which include temperature controls, are also available. These are recommended over regular hot rock heaters; adjustment of the surface temperature can be important.

Heat Strips and Pads (Flexwatt Heat Tape)

When heating a large number of enclosures on shelves, Flexwatt heat tape heating is recommended because of its low cost. At this time, heat tape systems are sold unassembled and require assembly, either by the store owner or by the customer.

Heat tape is normally used for heating seed trays in nurseries, and it comes in three widths and a corresponding wattage per foot (a low-heat 20 watt and a high-heat 40 watt). It is sold by the foot. This is an excellent and inexpensive source of bottom heat for all-glass vivaria. It creates an even low heat throughout most of the undersurface.

Heat strips should be placed underneath enclosures, making sure that the strip is not crushed or ripped by the edge of the enclosure. Use grooved shelves, or raise one end of the enclosure with a thin wood slat to prevent direct contact with enclosure bottoms that could damage the tape. Heat tape should always be connected to a rheostat, such as a light dimmer, or to a thermostatic control. For most species, heat tape should be used in conjunction with a spotlight over a basking area.

Heat tape should never be used on or applied to a vertical surface; the heat builds to potentially dangerous levels along the upper portion of the strip.

Reptile Heating Pads

Reptile heating pads are placed or adhered underneath enclosures to provide a heated area that can serve as a heating/basking site or to provide general heat, depending on location and heat output. As a rule, you should always leave at least half of the bottom of an enclosure unheated to allow self-regulation. Several brands of heating pads are available on the market, including Exo-Terra Heat Wave, T-Rex Cobra Mats, and Zoo Med ReptiTherm UTH. To make a decision, ask the advice of experienced herpetoculturists, whether hobbyists or store owners. Always follow directions for proper use, and check the temperature in the enclosure above the heated area after installation.

Place this type of pad under the vivarium carefully so that the vivarium edges and bottom surface do not crush the heating elements or thermostatic controls. These pads should be used only with a vivarium that has a recessed space underneath. Heat expansion may cause the glass bottom of a vivarium to crack if the control is set too high and the pad is in direct contact with the underside. The vivarium can also be placed on a wood frame (essentially lifting it above the pad) to create enough space to prevent these problems from occurring.

Ideally, reptile heat pads should be connected to a thermostatic control. Remember also that the type of substrate and the amount of substrate can act as an insulator and prevent heat from effectively reaching the surface. In some cases, this can lead to a buildup of heat beneath the enclosure that can cause the bottom glass to expand and crack. Take care to select a heating pad size that allows for a heat gradient in the vivarium. A heating pad that generates a high heat level and runs the length of a vivarium prevents the possibility of a cool temperature gradient.

Warm heat pads (particularly adhesive heat pads) without temperature control and in direct contact with the bottom of an all-glass vivarium can cause the bottom to expand and crack. With any heat pad, a temperature regulating device is highly recommended. Read the manufacturers' instructions to lessen the risk of fire or damage to a vivarium. Do not place a heat pad inside the vivaria. The only exception might be for use with a sick lizard. In this case, consult with an experience reptile veterinarian for proper use.

Although the common heating pads available in drugstores have been used successfully for heating vivaria in emergencies, they are not recommended for normal use.

Room Heaters

Many herpetoculturists use electric space heaters to maintain an adequate air temperature, particularly if they maintain large collections. This method is effective, but it is also expensive and can dramatically increase evaporative rates in vivaria, lowering relative humidity.

If you are keeping a large number of vivaria requiring similar ambient air temperatures, electric room heaters can be a simple way to maintain desired warmth in a room. This method is preferred by herpetoculturists with large collections. In winter, space heaters are often the only easy method of maintaining reptile rooms at adequate temperatures. They should be used with a backup space heater thermostat. Place room heaters in the middle of the room far from any flammable materials. Always follow manufacturer directions.

The cost of running electrical space heaters is high and is not economical unless you have a large number of vivaria. One major concern is the risk of overheated rooms resulting from thermostat variation or failure. A backup thermostat is highly recommended to help prevent this. Another consideration involves placement of the heater and thermostat(s) in the room. During winter, air along the floor is significantly cooler than at mid-room level. If a heater is placed on the floor, particularly if there is a ground-level draft (such as a door with a wide space along the bottom edge), the heater thermostat continuously reads a cool floor temperature, remains on, and ultimately overheats the room at mid-level and above. For reptiles, a 10-degree variation can mean life or death. Several herpetoculturists and commercial breeders have lost their entire collections because of a faulty heater or a mistake in the adjustment of the heater control. Another important consideration with space heaters is risk of fire. Many fires are caused every year by misused space heaters. Place heaters far away from any flammable materials, and follow directions very carefully. Once again, backup thermostats are highly recommended.

Pig Blankets

Pig blankets are large fiberglass-enclosed heating units that are available through feed stores and specialized reptile stores. They are primarily suitable with larger species and in large vivaria. It is important that the heat be controlled with a thermostat because surface temperatures can exceed 100°F. Pig blankets are ideal for setting up outdoor enclosures and for keeping a heated section or shelter during the cold winter months.

Pig blankets should be used according to instructions to prevent the risk of fire or overheating. Do not cover the surfaces of these units. They should be used, exposed, inside an enclosure. Failure to connect a pig blanket to a thermostat can result in overheating and damage to animals' ventral skin. If buried under a flammable substrate, they can present a risk of fire.

The Right Temperature for Your Lizard

Your lizard's temperature requirements will depend on where it is from. There are currently several books on the market, some species specific, that provide information on the temperature requirements of various lizards. Unfortunately, many of the lizard species sold in the trade are not covered in these books. And, unfortunately, some of the temperature ranges suggested by the authors are wrong. In many cases, you will have to find a temperature range that works based on your personal observations of your lizard's behavior in captivity.

The first step to finding the proper temperature range for your lizard is to look for information on its country of origin and habitat, if possible. Try to find this information before you buy a lizard. Remember that most countries have varied landscapes with many different temperature ranges. An animal living in a tropical country is actually exposed to cool temperatures if it comes from high altitude, montane areas. High altitude habitats are also subject to greater day and night fluctuations in temperature than lower elevation habitats are. For example, numerous lizards that were once imported by the tens of thousands from Chile were actually high-altitude lizards and probably required significant day

Lizards who bask in their natural environment require the opportunity to bask in their vivaria.

and night temperature variations to fare well. Many of these lizards died within a few months in captivity. Animals that live near the ground of primary tropical forest or under the canopy of tropical forest are exposed to significantly cooler temperatures than are those living along the edges of forest clearings.

During the course of your research, some field guides or research papers may provide important information on an animal's habitat. Geography books may also provide you with useful general temperature parameters. However, if you have just bought one or more lizards and you need to make some quick decisions as to vivarium design, the general information listed below may help.

Herpetoculturists establish gradients along the following general guidelines. These guidelines should be modified as you find out more information about the species you have purchased.

Desert and semi-arid area species:
Temperature nearest basking spot: 95°F to 100°F (35°C to 37.8°C)

Temperature farthest from spotlight: low to mid-80s F (27.2°C to 30°C)

Nighttime temperatures: 70s F (21°C to 26°C)

Winter: Temperate desert species should be hibernated; otherwise, daytime temperatures should be dropped 5 to 10 degrees F (2.8 to 5.5 degrees C), with nighttime temperatures in the 60s F (15.6°C to 20.6°C) for two months.

Temperate species:
Temperature nearest spotlight: 90°F to 95°F (32.3°C to 35°C)

Temperature farthest from spotlight: high 70s to low 80s F (25°C to 28.3°C)

Nighttime temperature: 70s F (21°C to 26°C)

Winter temperatures: Should be hibernated (brumated); temperature should be 50°F to 60°F (10°C to 15.6°C) for two to three months.

Lowland tropical forest, cleared areas, and dry tropical forest species:

Temperature nearest spotlight: 90°F to 95°F (32.2°C to 35°C)

Temperature farthest from spotlight: low 80s F (26.7°C to 28.3°C)

Nighttime temperature: high 70s to low 80s F (25°C to 28.3°C)

Winter: Drop temperature 5 to 8 degrees F (2.8 to 4.4 degrees C) for one to two months.

Under canopy and ground level tropical forest species:

Temperature nearest spotlight: 85°F to 90°F (29.4°C to 32.2°C)

Temperature farthest from spotlight: low to mid-80s F (28.9°C to 30°C)

Nighttime temperature: High 70s to low 80s F (25°C to 28.3°C)

Montane tropical species:

Temperature nearest spotlight: 80°F to 85°F (26.7°C to 29.4°C)

Temperature farthest from spotlight: mid- to high 70s F (25°C to 26.7°C)

Nighttime temperature: mid-60s F to low 70s F (17.8°C to 22.8°C)

Heating Control and Monitoring Equipment

The most widely used system for controlling heat in herpetoculture consists of light dimmers and rheostats. Light dimmers can be attached to lights as long as directions are followed. Many herpetoculturists have successfully used light dimmers on heat cables and other heating devices, such as heat tape. However, this is not the recommended usage for these products, and manufacturers do not stand behind their products if they are used in this way, in part because misuse increases the risk of fire. Although I'm not aware of fire-related problems associated with light dimmers used with heat cables or heat tape, connecting these devices to rheostatic devices is done at the user's risk. Other temperature-controlling instruments are available, such as thermostats, although they are more expensive.

Thermostats

Most thermostats work by simply switching a heating or cooling unit on or off until the appropriate temperature is reached and maintaining the temperature within a few degrees, sometimes within one degree, if the thermostat is sensitive enough. Simpler versions, such as wafer-type thermostats used on inexpensive poultry incubators or the thermostatic control of space heaters, require a thermometer to adjust the temperature. You can turn the dial to a certain number, but without a separate thermometer, you will not be able to accurately assess the setting of the thermostat. Currently, some commercial thermostats (such as Custom Reptile Network) allow you to set the temperature as well as the times when the temperature levels must be raised or lowered.

There are also pulse-proportioned control thermostats (e.g., Helix Controls) that essentially dim the heat to the right temperature instead of turning a heating device on and off. This type of thermostat is useful for heat cables and strips, for more even heating with incandescent bulbs, and for use in incubators.

Thermometers

Thermometers are essential for properly assessing the temperature in vivaria. The least expensive versions for vivaria are the adhesive, thermal-sensitive strips sold as high-range thermometers by some distributors. Unlike aquarium strip thermometers, which measure a relatively narrow range, high range thermometers indicate lower and higher temperatures—information required in the keeping of many reptiles. However, strip-type thermometers are not very accurate. Standard thermometers, such as wall-hanging thermometers or glass thermometers, can also be used in vivaria. The wall-hanging types tend to take up considerable space, and the glass thermometers are sometimes difficult to read.

A good thermometer for reptile keepers is the electronic digital readout variety, with a remote probe. An indoor switch position gives you a reading where the unit is placed, and the outdoor position gives you a reading wherever the probe is placed. Thus, if a digital thermometer is placed in a room, the probe can provide a reading of the inside of the vivarium. If the thermometer is placed inside a vivarium, the probe could give a reading of the surface of a basking site. Some of the more sophisticated digital thermometers provide daily minimum and maximum temperature readings; others include an alarm system, which gives a warning when the temperature gets too warm or too cool. These thermometers are invaluable with incubators or whenever careful monitoring of temperature is required. Digital readout thermometers are now readily available in the reptile trade.

The best thermometer for keeping reptiles is an infrared temperature gun, a device that measures surface temperatures without contact. It's basically a point-and-measure tool that will allow you to assess with some accuracy the temperature of different areas in an enclosure or the surface body temperature of a lizard. It can also measure the egg or substrate surface temperature in incubation containers. In short, it's one of the most valuable tools available to reptile keepers. The first ones offered on the market were expensive ($250+) but the price has dropped drastically, with small units now affordable at $25 or less.

CHAPTER 12

COOLING

D epending on a room's ambient temperature, some species of lizard may need to be cooled. Others may require a cool period to induce brumation (similar to hibernation), which may be a prerequisite to breeding.

Annual Cooling and Hibernation

As a general rule, species from tropical areas should be slightly cooled for one to two months during the winter, and usually kept drier during this period. Imported species from the southern hemisphere may need to be cooled during the summer. For tropical species, a drop of 5 to 8 degrees F (2.8 to 4.4 degrees C) is usually adequate. For tropical montane species, a 10-degree F (5.5-degree

Gravid long-nose dwarf chameleons (*Calumma gallus*) show bright blue "threat spots" on the head to deter males.

Most reptiles do not hibernate in the true sense. Even though their metabolism slows down considerably, they often continue to perform various activities, such as drinking and some moving about. For this reason, herpetologists use the words *brumate* (verb) and *brumation* (noun) when referring to this process, as distinct from *hibernation*. However, I propose that the more popular terms *hibernate* and *hibernation* be expanded to encompass the cooling period usually called brumation in herpetology:

hibernation: 1. a popular term used by herpetoculturists in reference to the winter cooling of amphibians and reptiles in captivity, usually associated with reduced activity and fasting. 2. the process of being subject to reduced winter temperatures and associated with limited activity and fasting (used by herpetoculturists with reference to amphibians and reptiles).

C) drop for about two months is often used by herpeto-culturists. For temperate species, drop the temperature 15 to 20 degrees F (7.7 to 10.5 degree C) for at least two months during the winter.

During this cooling period, animals from tropical countries usually feed less, whereas animals from temperate countries will not feed at all. Regularly monitor your lizards during this cooler period. Animals that show significant weight loss or look ill should be returned to normal temperatures and treated, if necessary. Always make water available to animals in hibernation.

Some species of insect-eating lizards require relatively cool temperatures all the time (thus, excess heat may become a problem). These include certain species of true chameleons; some of the Chilean species, which require cool night temperatures; and a number of montane species. When in doubt as to why a lizard is not faring well, establish a cool gradient to allow an animal to select cooler temperatures. If you live in a warm climate, it may become necessary to lower the temperature in your vivarium at times.

As a general rule, lizards from temperate climates should be hibernated during the winter for a period of two to four months. To confirm the need for hibernation, examine the range maps of the species you are keeping, and determine the winter temperatures. For lizards from areas where daytime aboveground temperatures are in the 60s F (15.6°C to 20.6°C) with a more significant drop in temperature at night, a slight drop in temperature (5 to 8 degrees F [2.8 to 4.4 degrees C]) during the winter months may increase the chances of breeding certain tropical species.

General temperature guidelines for hibernating and cooling lizards are as follows:

Temperate lizards: Cool temperate lizards to 50°F to 60°F (10°C to 15.6°C). Species from areas where it gets very cold can be hibernated down to the high 40s F (8.3°C to 9.4°C). Do not use spotlights.

Borderline subtropical species: Up to a 10-degree F (5.5-degree C) drop during the day while retaining a lower wattage spotlight over a basking area. Use a 10 to 15 degree F (5.5 to 7.7degree C) drop at night.

Subtropical species: 5 to 10-degree F (2.8 to 5.5 degree C) drop during the day while retaining a spotlight. Use a similar temperature drop at night.

Note: Hibernation or cooling during the winter should always be accompanied by a reduction in photoperiod to ten to eleven hours of exposure to light per day. If you want to keep southern hemisphere species under conditions that simulate their climatic and photoperiodic patterns, then adjust accordingly.

Cooling Methods
The following sections present a number of different cooling methods that are used (with varied applications) by herpetoculturists.

Cool Rooms
A commonly used method for keeping lizards that require cool temperatures is to keep them in the coolest area of the house, in either a basement, a garage, or a shaded room with a temperature range suitable for the species. In addition, some herpetoculturists insulate a room and install a

fan in a partially opened window or in an opening through a side wall. The fan is put on a timer so that cool air blows in at night. During the day, the fan is kept off; the insulation helps retain the cooler temperature.

Use a thermometer to assess that the temperature is within the desired range. Be aware that during the winter in cold areas of the United States, an unheated basement or garage can have temperatures at or even below freezing. This cool room method is commonly used by herpetoculturists who wish to hibernate their lizards.

Cool Packs

Cool packs can be bought at camping stores or supermarkets. The packs are placed in the freezer overnight and then used to maintain cool temperatures for extended periods of time. Purchasing a number of cool packs enables you to rotate them on a 24-hour basis. Use one by placing it under a thin metal container or a shelter, thus creating a cool gradient for terrestrial lizards. Cool packs are also useful when shipping lizards during the hot summer months.

Air Conditioners

Refrigerated air conditioning is the system preferred by most herpetoculturists for keeping species of amphibians and reptiles that require cool temperatures. Usually this means having a room devoted to the keeping of these species. Insulating the room can significantly reduce the cost of running the unit. Some individuals use flexible hoses (such as those used to vent clothes dryers) to direct the air flow from an air conditioning unit to the enclosures of species requiring cooler temperatures.

Wine Coolers

Refrigeration units designed specifically for cooling wines are available. Although relatively expensive, one great advantage of these units is that they are designed for maintaining temperatures of 54°F to 62°F (12.2°C to 16.7°C), temperatures that are coincidentally suitable for the hibernation of many species. Most units are also available with glass doors, which allow for a high degree of visibility. These units allow for the safe hibernation of animals indoors, even in warm climates. Sources for these include mail order catalogs, specialty wine stores, and the telephone directory.

CHAPTER 13
LIGHTING

F or most lizards, at least one source of light is required; two are generally preferable. Light is important for both temperature control (see chapter 11, Heating) and for creating a healthful environment for the lizards.

Incandescent Lighting (Tungsten Lightbulbs)

Standard incandescent bulbs or spotlights (preferable) in a reflector-type fixture are the most effective method of lighting as well as generating heat over a basking site. These bulbs with reflectors are essential for creating the temperature gradients required by many diurnal lizards to thermoregulate under vivarium conditions. For primarily

This cageless setup provides one source of light.

nocturnal lizards, such as most geckos, a low-wattage red bulb can provide heat without the brightness that these animals typically avoid (see chapter 11, Heating). A key to proper use is selecting the correct wattage to achieve the desired temperature at the basking site.

UVA and UVB Lighting

Many lizards benefit from the exposure to ultraviolet A and ultraviolet B radiation. In herpetoculture, these are provided by UV-generating bulbs. The benefit of UVB exposure is that it hypothetically allows many species of lizard that normally bask in nature to synthesize vitamin D_3, which is required for the absorption of calcium. Without adequate D_3, calcium will not readily be absorbed. In captivity, dietary vitamin D_3, usually in the form of a vitamin-mineral supplement, is often used as a substitute for sunlight or UV exposure. However, it is difficult to assess the right amount without oversupplementing, which can cause metabolic bone disease or calcinosis. Hypothetically, many lizard species can self-regulate D_3 production from UVB exposure. For this reason, allowing lizards to bask under a UV source as needed is con-sidered by many to be a safer and better alternative to D_3 supplementation.

Metabolic bone disease caused by calcium deficiencies is one of the most common health problems in captive lizards; having a means to assure proper D_3 levels is important to serious hobbyists.

UVA exposure can also have positive effects on breeding and behavior. Recent studies have shown that several lizard species have ultraviolet-sensitive vision and that UVA may be important for the herpetoculture of such species as anoles and desert iguanas because the UVA enhances visual cues (throat fan in male anoles and pore secretions of desert iguanas) associated with reproduction (Alberts 1994).

Successful breeding (high rates of egg fertility and hatching) of Madagascar leaf-tailed geckos (*Uroplatus fim-briatus*) at the Fort Worth Zoo increased dramatically fol-lowing regular exposure to BL (high UVA) blacklights (Stephen Hammack, pers. comm.).

To determine which bulbs you should use, you must first obtain some information on the natural behavior of your lizards. Lizards from savannah or desert areas that bask in the open benefit most from exposure to high-intensity reptile UVB lights, specifically mercury vapor bulbs or high reptile UVB fluorescent bulbs placed at less than a foot from basking sites. For forest or arboreal lizards that inhabit areas of dappled sunlight, reptile fluorescent UVB bulbs—not mercury vapor bulbs—are the best choice.

We do not know that all species of lizards effectively synthesize D_3 when exposed to UVB, but for the many that do, do not combine large amounts of dietary D_3 and UV exposure. This can lead to hypervitaminosis, metabolic bone disease, or calcinosis, ultimately causing death. For some species, it may be best to completely eliminate dietary D_3 when using UVB bulbs. However, because we know so little about the dietary needs of most lizards, continue to offer light D_3 supplementation (a light dusting of a reptile calcium supplement) once a week even when supplying UV exposure.

UV-Generating Fluorescent Bulbs

There are now a number of brands of UVA- and UVB-generating fluorescent bulbs sold in the reptile trade. Several, such as the widely used Zoo Med ReptiSun 5.0 bulbs, have been tested and shown to provide enough UVB for lizards to synthesize vitamin D_3 as long as they are used correctly and at a short distance (less than 12 inches) from basking lizards.

Place UV-generating bulbs on top of the vivarium screen in a high-quality reflector-type fluorescent fixture. Yearly replacement is recommended to assure high efficiency. Most of these bulbs also generate a fair amount of UVA, which has been shown to have beneficial effects on breeding behaviors and general activity levels. UV-generating bulbs are a good choice for species that live in partial shade for year-round exposure to a low and safe level of UVB. They are also a good choice for many arboreal species that will climb and bask at a close distance from the bulbs.

For desert species, two or more of these bulbs should be used over short vivaria. Because they generate little heat, they are safe to use without concern of overheating. Lizards require an additional heat source, such as a heat emitter or incandescent bulb, over a basking site.

UVB-Generating Mercury Vapor Bulbs

The most efficient UVB- and UVA-generating bulbs sold in the reptile trade are specially designed mercury vapor bulbs such as T-Rex Active UVB bulb. These bulbs are self-ballasted and should be placed in fixtures with deep dome reflectors and ceramic bases. It is important that the bulb not make contact with the vivarium screen. One option is to use reflectors on photographic light stands, allowing illumination from above the vivarium.

Because these bulbs have a high UVB output, it is critical to provide animals with a shaded or sheltered area so that they can regulate their exposure. Failure to do so can lead to skin or eye damage. Place bulbs on timers set for four to six hours a day. Although some believe that these bulbs can serve as both a heat and a UVB source, I recommend setting a UVB bulb on a timer for a few hours a day and providing an incandescent bulb for heat the rest of the day. These bulbs are also valuable in the treatment of metabolic bone disease in conjunction with the administration of calcium.

UVB-generation mercury vapor bulbs are the best choice with many desert and savannah species, but their use should be limited to just a few hours a day with forest lizards.

Warning

There is presently some medical concern that humans are being exposed to too much UV from fluorescent light sources and that this can be harmful to skin and eyes. Reflectors or other protective shields should be used with any UV-producing reptile bulbs to reduce exposure to humans. Take good care of your animals, but also be responsible and protect the people who will be in the same room as your reptile enclosures.

There is no substitute for natural light; if possible, allow your lizard to bask occasionally in the sun.

Red Lights

Low-wattage red incandescent bulbs will allow you to observe nocturnal animals at night. The nocturnal behavior of many lizards is unknown—much can be learned by observing species active at night with the use of these lights. Red incandescent bulbs can also be used to provide supplemental heat at night. Although the most readily available red bulbs are 25 watts, there are now higher-wattage red bulbs sold in the reptile trade and also available from stores specializing in lighting products.

Sunlight

Insect-eating lizards that bask in the open in the wild and bask under a spotlight in captivity can benefit from exposure to natural sunlight, even if only for a few hours per week. Exposure to sunlight is not generally recommended for species living under the canopies of primary forests

Shelter

Always provide shelters and shade when exposing animals to direct sunlight. Never leave lizards in a car in the sun with the windows closed. Infants and dogs have died from heat exposure in such vehicles, and so have amphibians and reptiles.

unless it is done for brief periods, either early or late in the day when sunlight is steeply angled and the temperature is moderate.

Herpetoculturists fortunate enough to live in areas with good weather most of the year can provide their sun-loving lizards regular exposure to sunlight by keeping them in outdoor vivaria with screen tops. Include plants and shelters to provide shade. Use a shadecloth (60 percent) screen for animals that do not bask in direct sunlight in open areas. During the warm months, herpetoculturists who keep their lizards indoors can transfer their lizards (for a few hours a day) into outdoor vivaria with screen tops, or even screen-sided enclosures, and plants and shelters. Never use glass-sided enclosures in the sun. As sunlight passes through glass, enough heat can be generated to quickly kill your lizards.

If you can't provide the proper type of outdoor vivarium or a screen-sided vivarium placed in front of an open window (remember that sunlight through window panes also generates heat), then forego exposing your lizards to natural sunlight. Most species of lizards fare well in captivity under artificial lights. Every year dozens, possibly hundreds, of lizards are killed by well-intentioned owners attempting to provide their lizards with sunlight. Usually the lizards die because of overheating, either because they were kept in glass enclosures or because of failure to provide shade and shelters.

Photoperiod

The photoperiod is the duration of an animal's daily exposure to light. Lizards in the wild are exposed to seasonal variations in the photoperiod. In many species, this plays an important role in reproduction, particularly in species from temperate and subtropical areas. With most species, herpetoculturists generally set their lights on timers and establish a photoperiod cycle of thirteen to fourteen hours of light and ten to eleven hours of darkness daily. During the winter or cooling period, the photoperiod is reversed, with ten to eleven hours of light and thirteen to fourteen hours of darkness. By manipulating the photoperiod, herpetoculturists have been able to increase the breeding frequency of certain species. Others have varied the photoperiod to increase the growth rate of baby lizards by creating shorter day and night cycles, such as eight-hour days and six-hour nights, to stimulate the lizards to feed more frequently.

Note: Animals living near the equator are subject to diminished variation in the photoperiod. The farther one goes from the equator, the greater the seasonal photoperiod variation.

CHAPTER 14

RELATIVE HUMIDITY AND VENTILATION

elative humidity is a measure of the degree of water vapor saturation in the air. The measurement of relative humidity is accomplished with an instrument known as a hygrometer. Relative humidity and ventilation are important (although often ignored) considerations when keeping various insect-eating lizards.

Desert lizards kept at high relative humidity levels with little ventilation can develop a number of diseases, from respiratory infections and bacterial skin infections to various mycoses (fungal infections). Rain forest lizards kept at low relative humidity levels become stressed, dehydrate rapidly, and have shedding problems. Water loss occurs during protein metabolism and especially during breathing, when a considerable amount of moisture can be lost to the air, particularly at low levels of relative humidity. Many insect-eating lizards fare well if they are maintained on a dry substrate with water available in a dish; however, there are numerous exceptions.

In the wild, natural shelters usually provide moderate-to-high relative humidity niches. The upper surface of a rock or a piece of wood provides a barrier that reduces air flow under the shelter and thus loss of water to the outside air. Delays in the rates at which rocks heat and cool also result in condensation of water on rock surfaces during the early morning hours. Anyone who has lifted a rock or a piece of wood when hunting for reptiles has noticed that the ground is usually damp under the rock or wood. An amphibian or reptile sheltered there does not dehydrate as rapidly and essentially finds itself in a high relative humidity chamber, compared with the outside air. An animal hiding in such a shelter has access to a level of relative humidity that helps soften the skin and facilitate shedding. In general, a shelter placed high above the ground provides a lower relative humidity than one on or near the ground.

Some of the challenges encountered in housing certain desert geckos lie not in keeping them dry enough but in providing enough humidity in their shelters to reduce dehydration and to facilitate shedding. This is the case with frog-eyed geckos (*Teratoscincus*) and tropical forest geckos, such as the bent-toed geckos (*Cyrtodactylus*) and cat geckos (*Aeluroscalabotes*). These species do not fare well at a low relative humidity. Most true chameleons fare best at a relative humidity in the 60 to 80 percent range.

Raising Relative Humidity

The easiest way to provide high relative humidity in a vivarium is to design one that contains water, either in the substrate or in a water container. As the water evaporates, the

A long-nose dwarf chameleon laps water from a leaf. Spraying foliage can provide both drinking water and adequate humidity.

relative humidity increases. If you have a naturalistic vivarium with two substrate layers, a lower layer consisting of pebbles for drainage and an upper layer of moist medium, the evaporation of water from the medium raises relative humidity. One of the most common ways of raising relative humidity is to mist the vivarium at least twice daily. The evaporation of droplets raises relative humidity; the substrate also absorbs some moisture and releases it over time.

As an alternative, misting systems on timers can be installed by connecting tubing and misters (available for landscape drip irrigation systems) to the plumbing of your home. A drain must be installed at the bottom of the vivarium to allow for drainage of excess water. This is easier than it sounds and is recommended if you are keeping large collections of certain lizards, such as some of the true chameleons. Many species fare better when provided with higher relative humidity and with misted water on a twice-daily basis.

Another method of raising relative humidity in a vivarium is to partially cover the top of the vivarium. As water evaporates from the substrate or water container, the rate at which water vapor particles escape the vivarium is reduced, and a greater density of vapor accumulates. It is important that only part of the vivarium be covered. If you reduce air flow too much, accumulating moisture can encourage the development of possibly life-threatening fungi and bacteria.

Sufficient humidity is essential for proper shedding, shown here.

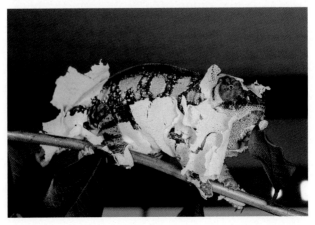

In areas with dry, warm climates, cool-air humidifiers can effectively cool down as well as raise the relative humidity of vivaria. They are recommended when keeping many of the tropical forest lizards (including true chameleons) and certain geckos (such as bent-toed geckos) in areas with an unusually dry climate. It is important that you carefully read instructions as to the proper maintenance of these humidifiers to prevent dangerous bacterial or fungal contamination over time. Many herpetoculturists have had extremely good results using these humidifiers with a number of more delicate species that require high humidity and cool-to-moderate temperatures.

Lowering Relative Humidity

If you live in a high relative humidity climate and are having problems keeping desert reptiles, the following steps help lower relative humidity.

In the room where you are keeping desert reptiles, keep windows closed and use a dehumidifier. Refrigerated air conditioners also lower relative humidity. When using low (16 inches high) vivaria in a room with moderate relative humidity, the simple use of spotlights over a vivarium creates a greater evaporative rate or lower relative humidity, particularly if there is no additional source of moisture in the vivarium or the room.

General Guidelines for Relative Humidity

Most lizard species fare well at a moderate relative humidity of 55 to 70 percent. For desert and semi-arid species, relative humidity should be less than 60 percent. Although many desert species tolerate a relative humidity up to 70 percent, others require a relative humidity of 40 percent or less. The relative humidity of deserts varies greatly according to location, from near coastal areas to deeply inland. Get as much information as possible on the species you are keeping.

Lizard species from tropical forests fare best at a relative humidity of 70 to 80 percent, and some rain forest species may require a relative humidity of 85 to 90 percent. Always

Large screen enclosures provide the airflow required for keeping panther chameleons (*Furcifer pardalis*) healthy.

Large screen enclosures provide the airflow required for keeping panther chameleons (*Furcifer pardalis*) healthy.

provide good ventilation in enclosures with a high relative humidity.

Ventilation

In terms of vivaria, when we speak of ventilation, we are not referring to a significant degree of air flow, such as a draft, but rather to areas of air exchange—between air inside the vivarium and air outside the vivarium. With most species, vivaria that have screen tops provide adequate ventilation. However, tall vivaria, in which the area for air exchange (screen top) relative to the total area of the vivaria is small, require additional ventilation (screen) on at least one side. An alternative is to use miniature fans, such as ones used for cooling electronic equipment, and placing them on the screen top or a side screen. These can be found in electronic stores (used electronic parts stores are sometimes another inexpensive source). Vivaria that are large, with significant sections of water, also benefit from the use of these fans. By placing a fan at different points in the viavarium, you create areas of varying dehydration rate, such as might be found in nature when wind provides a greater dehydrating effect at upper tree levels than it does closer to the ground.

There is considerable room for experimenting with ventilation, particularly in testing for preference when given a range of ventilation levels. Providing experimental vivaria with different ventilation variations may provide a tool for determining the environmental requirements of animals for which we presently have little information.

CHAPTER 15

FEEDING

There is still a lot to learn regarding the diets of lizards in captivity. In fact, relatively little is known about the actual nutritional requirements of most lizard species. The principles of feeding insect-eating lizards employed by most herpetoculturists are the result of relatively few scientific studies, plus considerable experimentation and observation by hobbyists and zoo personnel. Although we don't always know the reasons these methods work, improved health and longevity, as well as increasing success at captive breeding, suggest that the underlying assumptions and principles must be essentially correct.

Misconceptions exist as to the role of feeding in relation to an animal's health. By itself, feeding is not enough to assure the long-term survival of a lizard in captivity. Before the issue of feeding is addressed by hobbyists, other aspects of maintenance must be taken care of, including: selection of an adequate enclosure; a heat source, as well as a heat gradient within the enclosure; the right kind of lighting; the right kind of landscaping; the right level of relative humidity; adequate ventilation; and water. When all of these conditions are correct, the probability of an animal feeding, putting on weight, and faring well increases. Feeding is not a priority for a lizard that is stressed from cold, heat, anxiety, or thirst.

The Staples
Commercially raised insects should be the diet staple for most insect-eating lizards. In recent years, several species of commercial bred insects have become available in the pet trade, the fish bait trade, and through biological supply houses. As a rule, commercially raised insects can provide a good basic diet for a wide variety of these lizards, once

the insects are nutrient-loaded and dusted with a vitamin-mineral supplement.

Other food alternatives include field-collected insects and spiders (some Europeans call these field plankton), which can be obtained by beating grasses and other plants in fields or meadows and then running through with an insect net. But if you are busy and limited for time, commercially raised and readily obtainable insects are the easiest and most logical. In addition, you can never be sure that insects collected in the field do not contain agricultural chemicals that could have a harmful effect on your animals.

Be sure you are providing your lizard with the correct type of food in the correct amounts.

It's popular to say that "you are what you eat." But if you are a predator, like a reptile, you are also what your prey eats. Every time a lizard eats an insect in the wild, it consumes the insect plus any plant or animal contents in the intestine of that insect. This is nature's way for the lizard to get its meat and veggies all in one neat packet. The contribution of insect gut contents to the diet of an insectivorous lizard should not be ignored. This can be a means of providing important vitamins and minerals as well as plant compounds, which can contribute to the animal's health, well-being, and brightness of coloration.

Commercially Raised Insects

The following is information on commercially obtainable insects, which should form the staple of your insect-eating lizard's diet. None of these insects should simply be fed to your lizard as you purchased them from a store. Always gut load insects before feeding them to your lizard.

Gray Crickets (Acheta domestica)

These are the commercially bred and readily available crickets of the pet trade. They are now carried by most stores that specialize in reptiles. They can also be obtained through fish bait mail order sources. For most lizards, these should be the first choice as a staple of an insectivore diet. They can be ordered in a variety of sizes, from pinheads to six-week-old winged adults. This means that a suitable size can be obtained for feeding most insect-eating lizard species. Crickets are easily digested by most lizards.

Mealworms (*Tenebrio molitor*)

Mealworms are the most widely sold insects in the pet trade. They can be kept for weeks in a plastic container (with air holes) stored in a refrigerator or a cool area of the house. Serious hobbyists should consider culturing mealworms. They can be maintained and raised in large plastic boxes or tubs filled with an inch of oat bran or corn flour. Before being used, the bran or flour should be baked in shallow pans in an oven at 200°F (93.3°C) for 20 minutes to kill off grain mites. Layers of newspaper or cloth can be placed on top of this layer for easy collecting. Provide pieces of carrot or squash and banana peel as a source of water.

One advantage to culturing your own mealworms is that you eventually have them in a variety of sizes to suit your animals' needs, instead of having only the standard medium size offered in many pet stores. Two- to five-week-old meal-worms can be invaluable for feeding smaller lizards; adult mealworms should be fed only to the larger species of lizard. Another great advantage to raising mealworms yourself is that you are able to offer your lizards "white" soft-bodied mealworms that have just molted; these are more easily digested than adult mealworms are. Recently, the use of meal-worms as a lizard food has fallen into disfavor because the tough chitinous exoskeleton makes them relatively difficult for smaller lizards to digest. All hobbyists have seen a lizard stuff itself on mealworms one day and regurgitate the entire meal the following day. Feeding smaller mealworms, smaller quantities of mealworms at a time, and white mealworms reduces the incidence of such problems.

In general, mealworms should be offered as part of a varied insect diet, which for many lizard species consists primarily of crickets. But this is not a hard-and-fast rule. Diets should be adjusted according to the lizard species. Larger lizards, whose jaws are capable of cutting through the exoskeleton, fare better with a higher percentage of mealworms in their diet than do

Crickets are a popular staple for many insect-eating lizards.

smaller lizards. The only suitable mealworms for feeding small lizards are correspondingly tiny ones, whose exoskeletons are likely to be torn by the smaller lizards' jaws. Offer only in small quantities.

Mealworms in various stages of development can also be useful as a part of the diet for certain species. With lizards that recognize prey by scent (such as some of the skinks), mealworm pupae can be offered as food. Mealworm beetles can be a valuable food source for some species of lizards, such as the toad-headed agamid (*Phrynocephalus mystaceus*), although many other lizards will not touch them. Mealworms will eventually turn into beetles if kept moderately warm.

Caution: Do not feed more mealworms than your lizard can eat. Hungry mealworms can injure and even kill small lizards that are sleeping on the ground. Mealworms have been implicated in injuries to toes and damage to the cloacal and dorsal-pelvic areas. To reduce the chance of these types of prey injuries, offer only as many mealworms as your lizard is likely to eat, and place a small piece of carrot in the enclosure for uneaten mealworms to feed on.

Giant mealworms and common mealworms are eaten by a variety of insect-eating lizards. Do not overfeed.

King Mealworms (*Zophobas morio*)

These resemble mealworms, although they are larger and have somewhat softer bodies. Requiring higher temperatures for maintenance, they are best kept stored at room temperature. They can be maintained like mealworms, except they have a greater need for warmth; they also require more vegetable matter as a source of moisture. Some of the larger species of lizards (such as adult tokay geckos, basilisks, and water dragons) have successfully been maintained long term on diets consisting primarily of supplemented king mealworms and immature mice.

If these worms are left loose in a vivarium, they can become a problem. They readily eat any eggs they come across, and they can cause injuries or even death to torpid smaller reptiles.

Wax Worms (*Galleria mellonella*)

Wax worms tend to be fatty and are not recommended as a basic diet for most insect-eating lizards. They can, however, serve as a valuable component in a varied insect diet. They can also help lizards put on weight. Many lizards that are reluctant to feed on other insect species will start feeding on wax worms. Although distributors claim this to be a low chitin insect (the implication being it should be easily digestible), wax worms do have an exoskeleton that is, in fact, not easily digested by many species of lizard. Thus, they

Roaches are a newly available food item for some lizards.

should be offered as food only in small numbers per feeding, or you will be faced with the same regurgitation syndrome mentioned regarding mealworms. As with mealworms, pupae and the adult moths can be a useful food source for some lizards.

Wax worms should be stored in pine shavings in a plastic-covered box and kept stored in a cool area of the house. These are not readily available from most pet stores. They are often most easily obtained through fish bait mail order businesses.

Roaches

In recent years, the availability of a variety of commercially bred, nonpest roaches has expanded the food options for raising lizards. The fact that several roach species do not fly or climb and are easily raised in glass or plastic tubs has also allowed those keeping small collections to avoid weekly trips to buy or order crickets. The biggest obstacle to feeding roaches is likely their psychological association as invasive, creepy pests.

Roaches are very nutritious, appealing to a wide range of species, and can be fed a varied diet, including commercial roach diets, dog food, fruits and vegetables, and, for some species, even table scraps. Recommended fast-breeding nonclimbing and nonflying species are the false death head roach (*Blaberus discoidalis*) and the Guyana orange spotted roach (*Blaptica dubia*). An Internet search will provide sources of both roaches and related supplies.

Wingless Fruit Flies (*Drosophila melanogaster*)

Wingless fruit flies can be a valuable component in a varied diet for miniature species and their offspring. Larger fruit flies, such as *Drosophila hydei*, can be useful for rearing babies of certain species, including some of the true chameleons and smaller day geckos.

Cultures, as well as culture materials, for these tiny wingless flies can be obtained either through biological supply houses or through mail order live tropical fish food suppliers (look for ads in tropical fish magazines).

Snails (*Helix aspera*)

In moist habitats, snails can be a readily available, high-calcium prey item for a number of lizard species. I experimented offering the common edible snail (*Helix aspera*) to several types of lizards and found that some geckos, skinks, and monitors relished them. Snails are the preferred food of the popular pink-tongue skink (*Hemisphaeriodon gerrardii*), which can require a little work to convert to feeding on chicken-based cat food, a proven viable alternative. The larger leaf-tailed geckos (*Uroplatus fimbriatus* and *Uroplatus henkeli*) and chameleon anoles (*Chamaeleolis* species) are fond of snails. Healthy edible snails can be a good source of calcium and are useful to scent the food of specialized species by simply rubbing mucus over the intended prey. Snails can, however, carry parasites, notably protozoa. The best course is to raise these species under controlled conditions to minimize parasite loads. An alternative for snail specialists that will eat inert food, such as pink-tongue skinks, is to offer cooked snails, such as Can o' Snails by Zoo Med.

Pink Mice

But mice are not insects! True, but insect-eating lizards often eat them, and they do have a relatively high nutritional value. *Pink mice* or *pinkie mice* are common terms for newborn (hairless) mice.

One- to two-day-old mice are eaten by many species of medium to large insect-eating lizards. In fact, as far as most of these lizards are concerned, if it moves and it's not too big, then it's probably fair game. Pink mice should be used as an occasional meal, not as a staple diet, for insect-eating lizards. Mice are nutritious, but when only one or two days old, they are also calcium deficient for lizards (unless they are offered very soon after removal from the mother). Prior to feeding to lizards, the rumps of the mice should be dipped in calcium carbonate. Do not dip live mice head first or coat them with any vitamin mix as you would crickets. Calcium in the respiratory passages of a pink mouse causes distress and suffering, whereas a rump dipped in calcium does not. Pink or fuzzy mice may be too rich for many insect-eating lizards and may cause fatty degeneration of the liver if they are fed as a primary diet.

Pink mice can be obtained from rodent breeders and through stores specializing in reptiles. Mice are also easily bred in small numbers; a tank containing a group of one male with up to five females could provide at least fifty pink mice a month (more than the average hobbyist would need).

Some lizards will eat pink, or newborn, mice.

A crested gecko enjoys a cricket snack.

Herpetocultural Cuisine: Four Steps to Feeding Insects to Lizards

The proper feeding of lizards involves four steps: food selection, food preparation (gut loading), vitamin-mineral supplementation, and serving methods. Each can play an important role in the long-term health of your lizards.

Step 1: Food Selection

Although this is an important consideration when feeding lizards, it is one area in which many people lack good judgment.

Size

Errors in size selection of prey are probably the most common in the pet trade. For example, many pet stores selling green anoles (*Anolis*) sell only one size of cricket (five-week-old adults) and standard mealworms. Neither of these food items is the right size for the anoles; they are also inadequate for virtually every other small lizard sold. Yet when these are offered to a hungry anole, the lizard usually goes after the

Don't make the mistake of feeding your green anole overly large food items.

insect and struggles to swallow it. The next day, it may seem ill and bloated and often regurgitates. Insect-eating lizards are not snakes, and they are not monitor lizards. Most have evolved to eat many small prey items over the course of a day. Large prey has a smaller surface relative to its volume when compared with small prey. This allows a relatively smaller area for digestive juices to work on. In the digestive tract of a small lizard, a large insect prey item is a big object with a tough exoskeleton. More than likely it was not chewed before it was swallowed. Large prey ingested by an insect-eating lizard may start decomposing before it is digested, and the lizard that has eaten it may become ill and regurgitate the meal.

Another aspect of size selection involves the time it takes prey to pass through the digestive tract. Small insects are digested faster and move out of the stomach and through the digestive tract more quickly, thus allowing the lizard to eat again significantly sooner than when it is given large prey. Large insects can take up so much room in the stomach of a small lizard that the lizard's breathing is impaired.

How to gauge the right size insect to feed lizards is learned with experience. As a general rule, the width of the insect should be not more than one-third the width of the lizard's head. The length of the insect should be less than one and one-quarter times the length of the lizard's head, and the apparent volume of the insect no more than one-third the apparent volume of the lizard's head. Choose insect size based on the idea that it should take five insects to fill the belly area of the lizard.

For green anoles, the guidelines are slightly different. For subadult and adult green anoles, three-week-old crickets are suitable. These same crickets can also be fed to house geckos, many of the smaller day geckos, the smaller Chilean lizards now being imported, as well as baby green water dragons (*Physignathus cocincinus*).

Diet Selection

For most smaller species of lizards, appropriate-size crickets should be the primary food. If you raise mealworms, smaller white mealworms that have just molted can also be used. Mealworms can be a useful food for lizards as long as the right size is selected. Larger insect-eating lizards should be fed a varied diet of crickets, mealworms or king mealworms, and occasional pink mice. Some species may refuse the above yet will feed on cockroaches.

Certain species are specialized feeders and require experimentation to determine a suitable diet. For example,

Always gut load crickets and mealworms before offering them to your lizards.

the toad-headed agamid (*Phrynocephalus mystaceus*) often refuses most standard commercially raised insects yet readily consumes mealworms, beetles, and dewinged and stunted flies. There are also quite a few species not usually recommended for any but the most devoted and expert of herpetoculturists: lizards that are specialized ant feeders. These include most of the horned toads (*Phrynosoma*), several of the agamines, and the Australian spiny moloch (*Moloch horridus*), which thrives only on a diet of specific ant species.

Step 2: Food Preparation

You may think that all you have to do is go to a store, buy a plastic baggy of crickets, and dump them into the lizard tank. Unfortunately, this approach usually doesn't work if you want your lizards to live for several years. Most people who buy lizards from pet stores seldom keep them for more than a few months. In addition to other factors, they are typically not fed in the right manner.

Solutions for Retail Stores

One solution to the problem of nutrient-deficient insects for retail stores is to feed the insects an improved diet prior to selling them. This is actually a simple procedure. The following are some recommendations for improving the diet of the most commonly commercially raised insects.

There are now several diets for crickets and other feeder insects offered in the pet trade that will improve the insects' nutritional value and that can be used as a gut-loading diet. You can also feed crickets and mealworms the powdered remains found at the bottom of rodent chow bags or dog chow bags. Flaked baby cereals and ground oatmeal can also be used. Mix in powdered calcium carbonate. For crickets, offer slices of orange as a source of water. For mealworms, offer carrot or squash. Additionally, crickets should be offered a variety of greens and vegetables, such as grated squashes, carrots, kale, mustard greens, and finely chopped thawed mixed vegetables. Place the foods on a flat dish to prevent any moisture or water from spreading throughout the cricket enclosure.

Gut Loading

Most commercially sold insects are usually nutrient deficient (including vitamin and mineral deficient) for the purpose of feeding lizards. In brief, their guts are empty, and the insect body itself cannot provide all the nutritional requirements of lizards. Virtually all commercially raised insects sold in stores are calcium deficient. They may also be deficient in a number of vitamin precursors and vitamins, including beta-carotene, the B vitamins, vitamin C, and vitamin D_3, as well as minerals and trace elements. Plant pigments, which may contribute to an animal's brightness of color, may also be lacking. Indeed, the coloration of many captive insect-eating amphibians and reptiles does tend to fade in captivity.

Any hobbyist who buys insects on a regular basis should have plastic containers or bins in which to hold the insects for a couple of days prior to offering them. Some of the translucent plastic terrariums with lids that are sold in pet stores work quite well for this purpose.

The following methods work for gut nutrient loading and vitamin-mineral loading insects to be fed to lizards. Note that *gut loading* was a term that initially referred strictly to offering a high calcium diet to increase the calcium levels in feeder insects and balance their calcium-to-phosphorus ratio. Nowadays, gut loading is used to describe not only calcium loading of insects but also the general improvement of insects' nutritional value by feeding them a high-quality diet that includes select vitamins and minerals.

Gut Loading Schedule for Crickets, Mealworms, and Roaches

Day one: When you first obtain the insects, keep them without food or water for a day. The idea is to make them hungry so that they readily feed on what you are going to offer them.

Day two: Offer them one of the following: (1) a commercial gut-loading diet, of which there are several brands currently available; (2) pulverized rodent chow supplemented

Optional Food Preparation

Prior to the vitamin-mineral supplementation and offering of insects to lizards, many specialized hobbyists prepare the food in the following ways:

Catch crickets individually and pinch their "thighs," either with tweezers or by hand. This causes the crickets to drop their hindlegs, preventing the crickets from jumping out of the feeding dishes or moving around actively, thus slowing the rate at which the vitamin-mineral supplement coating is lost.

Mealworms can be pinched hard at midbody with fine tweezers or between thumb and forefinger. The result is partial paralysis of the back half of the mealworm. Here again, escape from a feeding dish is prevented. Another consideration is that pinched and injured mealworms that escape do not usually survive. This is particularly desirable in the case of king mealworms, especially in a vivarium where lizards are breeding.

One technique used with lizards that recognize prey by scent is to crush the heads of mealworms with tweezers. The result is a mealworm that smells right but doesn't move. This works well with lizards like baby monitors or Indonesian blue tongue skinks (*Tiliqua gigas*). These animals can spend so much time attempting to eat a single active mealworm that by the time they return to the dish, the others may have all escaped.

Although these preparations may sound cruel to insects, we are dealing with predators and must decide between the welfare of predator lizards and that of insect prey.

and blended with calcium carbonate or calcium gluconate; (3) tropical fish food flakes mixed with high-protein baby cereal flakes and calcium carbonate; or (4) fine ground oatmeal, barley, other grains, or sesame seed mixed with calcium carbonate. Offer this to insects one out of three feedings. For the other two feedings, offer insects a variety of fresh foods, preferably high in calcium. Vary the vegetables offered: mustard greens, collard greens, kale, cooked green beans, chopped mixed vegetables, Chinese cabbage, grated squashes, and grated or cooked carrots. Lightly sprinkle greens with calcium carbonate and mix in. Provide water to insects with a varied selection of slices of orange, the skin of yellow squash, and pieces of grated or cooked carrot.

Day three: Feed the insects to the lizards.

Step 3: Vitamin-Mineral Supplementation

When you don't have the time to nutrient load insects, the very least you should do is supplement the insects with vitamins and minerals. If you properly gut load feeder insects and provide your lizards with exposure to natural sunlight, minimal supplementation is required. Most of the commercial lizard breeders who keep their lizards outdoors and feed their insects a high-quality diet use little supplementation. If all other conditions are adequate, supplement once a week with powdered calcium carbonate and a general vitamin-mineral supplement that should contain some formed vitamin A. Recent research seems to indicate that it is probably best to avoid vitamin D_3 supplementation of basking lizards if they are regularly exposed to a UVB source, such as sunlight (Gary Ferguson, PhD, pers. comm.).

For lizards kept indoors with no exposure to sunlight, vitamin-mineral supplementation will depend on how your lizards are kept. If you use a UVB-generating bulb and

If you can't gut load feeder insects, at least dip them into a supplement before giving them to your lizards.

a good gut-loading regimen, calcium supplementation once or twice a week should be all that is necessary. The distance from the bulb to the animal is probably a critical factor. Unfortunately, we do not know enough about calcium metabolism in lizards (which appears to vary from species to species) to have pat answers about the best supplementation procedures.

If there is no exposure to a UVB source (sun or UVB bulbs), then calcium-vitamin D_3 supplementation once a week is recommended with most species of lizard, as long as they are fed high-quality, gut-loaded insects. With hatchlings and subadults, calcium-vitamin D_3 supplementation twice a week is recommended.

Without proper gut loading of insects, it will be necessary to resort to commercial vitamin-mineral supplements to correct deficiencies associated with nutrient-poor food insects. This is not completely without risk because most commercial reptile vitamin-mineral supplements are based on modified bird formulations, and their effect on various lizard species have not been supported with research. As a result, many of the commercial vitamin-mineral supplements tend to be high in vitamin A and, in some cases, vitamin D_3. Other vitamins probably are not present in the right proportions either. Ideally, a formulation will be developed that allows for regular dusting without the risk of overdosing—a very dilute vitamin-mineral supplement.

Dusting food insects once a week with a mixture of one part commercial vitamin-mineral reptile supplement with one part calcium carbonate is adequate for most adult insect-eating lizards. For immature animals, supplement twice a week. Depending on the species, this frequency may need to be adjusted. Many herpetoculturists choose to supplement lightly at each feeding. For this purpose, the T-Rex dusts (T-Rex Superfoods), which were developed specifically to balance the composition of crickets, have proven a good vitamin-mineral formula. Make adjustments if an animal shows signs of metabolic bone disease.

Unfortunately, because most lizard buyers are not willing to provide the right kind of lighting or provide their animals a varied diet, vitamin-mineral supplementation is critical for most lizards sold in the pet trade to fare well long term. One of the most common diseases in captive lizards, metabolic bone disease, is easily prevented with proper vitamin-mineral supplementation.

In spite of some of the recently uncovered problems with current commercial vitamin-mineral supplements, there is no doubt that the practice of vitamin-mineral supplementation by hobbyists has contributed significantly to the successful captive breeding and rearing of many lizard species. Therefore, some type of vitamin-mineral supplementation is recommended for the long-term survival of most insect-eating lizards in captivity.

Hypervitaminosis A

Larry Talent, PhD, at the University of Oklahoma, and Gary Ferguson, PhD, at Texas Christian University, have conducted research on the effects of specific vitamins on certain species of insect-eating lizards. Preliminary results of their ongoing research suggest a possible relationship between vitamin A, vitamin D_3, and calcium metabolism. Excess vitamin A in commercial reptile supplements may have a negative effect on several species of insect-eating lizards, notably certain species of true chameleons (e.g., *Chamaeleo johnstoni* and *Furcifer pardalis*), day geckos, and fat-tail geckos. Because of an interrelationship between ingested vitamin A, vitamin D_3, and calcium, it appears that in some species, too much vitamin A can indirectly lead to a depletion of calcium reserves, resulting in symptoms of metabolic bone disease. Other effects of hypervitaminosis A include excessive shedding and eye problems. Some of these effects can be offset by increasing the amount of vitamin D_3, but there is also a risk of administering too much vitamin D_3. Unfortunately, many of the reptile vitamin-mineral supplements presently available contain many times the amount of vitamin A required by most lizards. For species with low vitamin A tolerance, these vitamin-mineral supplements may prove detrimental over time. With vitamin A–sensitive species, some herpetoculturists choose to use only commercial vitamin-mineral supplements with beta-carotene (a vitamin A precursor) and a vitamin D_3 and calcium supplement. Any formed vitamin A is provided only through careful gut loading of insects.

Calcium Supplementation for Geckos
Many gecko breeders use special methods to provide large amounts of calcium to their animals because females of species that lay several clutches of eggs can become calcium depleted. One method is to make calcium carbonate or calcium gluconate powder (Rep-Cal) available at all times. Place the powder in a jar lid or small dish set on the substrate or on a platform in a gecko's vivarium. With species that are known to ingest sand regularly, such as *Teratoscincus*, calcium carbonate is added and mixed into the sand substrate. With species that are very prolific and have high calcium demands, such as the Madagascan ground gecko (*Paroedura picta*), calcium in liquid form or mixed with a watered-down baby food is administered individually with an eyedropper or syringe. Liquid calcium carbonate can be obtained by prescription from a pharmacy.

Until better methods are available, pet stores that recommend you buy vitamin-mineral supplements, even for the inexpensive green anole (*Anolis carolinensis*) that you have just bought, are not just out to make a buck. Their suggestions are based on the current practices of most lizard keepers.

Experimental Supplementation Techniques
Some breeders are currently experimenting with three vitamins to help determine their contribution to the overall health and captive breeding of insect-eating lizards: beta-carotene (a vitamin A precursor), vitamin C, and vitamin E. These supplementation techniques are experimental, and any claims as to possible benefits remain speculative. However, herpetoculturists have attributed a number of benefits to supplementing with these vitamins.

Beta-carotene may play a role in increased reproductive success, improved coloration, and prevention of eye and respiratory disorders. At one time, it was suggested that beta-carotene, in the form of grated carrots fed to insects or as a supplement, was probably the best and safest way to ensure that lizards get adequate amounts of vitamin A. The current view is that some formed vitamin A should be offered because experience and experimentation with some lizards, notably chameleons, indicates that for many lizard species, beta-carotene (hypothetically converted to vitamin A as needed) will not be an alternative to providing formed vitamin A. However, excess vitamin A may be harmful to certain species and may possibly impair long-term, multigenerational breeding.

Vitamin E may improve the likelihood of reproductive success with reptiles. In veterinary medicine, vitamin E in the diet has been shown to reduce or prevent steatitis, a condition resulting from excess consumption of unsaturated fatty acids. Typical symptoms of steatitis include massive accumulations of altered fat as well as the development of lesions under the skin and throughout the abdominal cavity.

Beta-carotene and vitamin E can be purchased in gelatin capsules at health food stores. Open the capsule, and hand dip the dorsal part of the insect into the contents and then into a mineral-vitamin mix prior to offering to your lizard. Beta-carotene is also available in a powder that can be added to the vitamin-mineral mix. Hobbyists generally offer this supplement once a week.

Vitamin C is present in the diets of most wild reptiles; it is probably obtained primarily from the gut contents of prey. A small amount of vitamin C in the diet may help prevent mouth rot (stomatitis). Other benefits have yet to be determined.

Crystal vitamin C can be purchased at a health food store, then placed in a small mortar and crushed with a pestle. Vitamins can also be crushed by placing them between two pieces of cardboard and pounding them with a hammer. Add a small amount of the finely powdered vitamin C to the vitamin-mineral mix for coating insects.

Supplementation Schedules
Many hobbyists vitamin-mineral supplement the insects they offer at every feeding, but it is possible to give too

much supplementation. As noted, the result can be hyper-vitaminosis or, in the case of excessive calcium-D$_3$ supplementation, mineralization of subcutaneous and visceral organs, usually as a result of calcium deposits. This type of metastatic calcification can result in premature death.

We do not yet have clear guidelines as to the actual vitamin-mineral requirements of most lizard species. As a rule (until better information comes along), the diet of juveniles (because of their rapid growth rate) should be supplemented more often than that of adults. Most herpetoculturists vitamin-mineral supplement the diet of juveniles every one to two feedings. Once the animal is mature and its growth rate has slowed down, supplementation is usually cut down to every third or fourth feeding. Another choice is to supplement the insects fed to adult lizards with a vitamin-mineral powder at one feeding per week and with calcium carbonate at a different feeding each week. For breeding females, herpetoculturists usually increase the schedule of calcium-vitamin D$_3$ supplementation or calcium carbonate. This ensures that she receives enough calcium for the formation of adequately calcified egg shells.

Don't just throw mealworms or crickets into the cage with lizards; they can hide, escape, or even injure lizards. Shown is a baby bearded dragon with a lesion caused by crickets.

During the breeding season, gecko breeders usually dust insects with calcium carbonate or a calcium-vitamin D_3 supplement at every feeding.

Freshness of Supplements

It is better to purchase smaller amounts of a fresh supply of a vitamin-mineral supplement than a large supply. A large container of vitamin-mineral supplement opened frequently (or with contents exposed to the air or high temperatures) will deteriorate over time until you are no longer able to assess the effectiveness of the vitamins. Fat-soluble vitamins, such as vitamins A and D_3, are prone to rapid deterioration. Read labels for expiration dates, buy smaller quantities, keep supplements in a cool place, and keep containers sealed tightly between uses.

Step 4: The Right Way to Serve Lunch

Most hobbyists, after swirling insects in a jar with a vitamin-mineral mix, simply dump the insects onto the floor of the vivarium. However, if you have only a few lizards and you put in too many insects at one time, the uneaten ones will scurry about the tank, losing their vitamin-mineral coating, and hide. Later, your hungry lizard will eat these escapee insects, which are now probably nutrient depleted and without the vitamin-mineral coating.

I have heard many stories of hobbyists who swear that they methodically vitamin-mineral coated their insects when feeding baby lizards and the lizards still didn't thrive. The cause is invariably the wrong calcium-phosphorus ratio or inadequate amounts of vitamin D_3 or, quite often, inappropriate feeding methods that allowed the introduced insects to lose their vitamin-mineral coating.

Rule No. 1: Never offer your lizards more than they will eat in one feeding. After observing your lizard for a period of time, you will be able to easily determine how many insects it will eat at each feeding. Some people with large collections have a very methodical way of feeding so that each vivarium gets a specific number of insects at each feeding.

Rule No. 2: Introduce coated insects in a feeding dish. The challenge is finding the right kind of dish. Unfortunately, no dishes sold in the pet trade, including the standard plastic watering dishes, are designed for feeding insects to reptiles. Finding the right dish will require a trip to an imported goods or department store in search of small porcelain or glass dishes. Import stores often sell small sauce dishes that work quite well for small lizards. The dish should be high enough to prevent the insects from crawling out but not so high that the lizards can't see the contents. Note: Crickets without hind legs and pinched mealworms will usually not be able to escape from smooth glass- or porcelain-sided dishes.

Forceps Feeding

Many lizards learn to take food offered them from forceps. One advantage of this type of feeding is that you can control the quantity of insects offered and eaten by a specific lizard during a feeding. In a community situation, where certain lizards may be dominant over others, this allows you to feed each lizard individually and ensure that all are adequately fed. The one disadvantage to forceps is that lizards will sometimes inadvertently clamp down on the forceps themselves, risking damage to the mouth and the possible development of stomatitis (mouth rot). Forceps can be purchased from medical supply houses and specialized reptile dealers.

Feeding Tubes

You can also create an insect feeding tube or jar. This can be made of bamboo, PVC pipe, or an empty coffee can. A feeding tube is essentially a container with a top to allow for the placement of insects and supplementation inside. About ¼ inch (6.4 mm) from the bottom, drill two holes, ⅜ to ½ inch (9.5 to 12.7 mm) in diameter. Fill the holes with small corks.

Before feeding, open the lid of the tube, and add a layer of vitamin-mineral mix that reaches the bottom of the punched holes. Place a number of coated insects inside the container. Close the lid, place inside the vivarium, and remove the cork plugs from the holes. The insects will struggle to get out, getting even more coated with the mixture. Eventually they will emerge, one at a time, from the container. Over time, lizards will become conditioned to feeding from the tube and wait to grasp an insect as it exits the feeding tube.

Feeding Schedules

Feeding schedules should be adjusted to the age and growth rate of your animal. Most juvenile lizards have a very rapid growth rate and thus require frequent feedings to build muscles and skeletons. They should be fed every one to two days. After growth slows down and levels off (between one and two years in most species), feeding should decrease to three times a week. Breeding females, particularly those laying several clutches of eggs during a breeding season, should be placed back on a one- or two-day schedule (see the following section). Take care to avoid obesity. A plump, rotund lizard is not a healthy lizard. Such animals may be incapable of breeding and may be destined to a shortened life span. Use your good judgment, and seek the advice of an experienced herpetoculturist or qualified reptile veterinarian.

Feeding Female Lizards During Their Breeding Cycles

For female lizards, the demands of reproduction mean a considerable investment of energy. Several species of insect-eating lizards lay multiple egg clutches, further taxing a female's energy reserves. Because the synthesis of egg shells requires calcium, significant demands are placed on the calcium reserves of gravid females. In captivity, failure to provide adequate calcium can result in soft- or thin-shelled eggs that are less resistant to trauma and disease. There is also evidence that the nutritional quality of the diet offered a female lizard can affect the size of eggs and the quality and quantity of food reserve available to the embryo (in the yolk). Poor health and inadequate diet are believed to be associated with an increased risk of egg binding in gravid females. Breeding and gravid females must be offered a high-quality, calcium-rich diet.

Sizes and types of food offered to gravid females are varied. Because the developing eggs may take up a significant portion of the abdominal cavity, the digestive organs may be compressed, thus making feeding on large prey or on a large volume of prey items impossible. Gravid female lizards will usually feed on smaller prey and ingest a smaller total volume of prey per feeding. Offer smaller prey more frequently.

Fungi and Fungal Toxins

It is very important that all food fed to insects be fresh and switched out regularly. Their enclosures should be kept clean. There is some evidence that insects that have consumed moldy food can harbor fungi and fungus-derived toxins, which could prove harmful or fatal to lizards. In the case of some fungal toxins (e.g., aflatoxins,) the effects may be cumulative. Keep food insects in a meticulous manner. Offer fresh food, and make sure it is not moldy.

Alternatives to Insects

Insect-eating lizards may also eat other types of food. A number of species, such as plated lizards, skinks, lacertids, teiids, and agamas, show varying degrees of omnivory and will feed on fruits. Others may feed on nectars or meats.

Plant Matter

Several species of insect-eating lizards will also feed on plant matter. Well-known examples are some of the larger agamines (such as bearded dragons and water dragons), basilisks, several species of skinks, plated lizards, several species of swifts, and several species of teiids (such as ameivas). Several gecko species will also feed on baby foods or nectars.

Consult the available literature to find out whether your lizard consumes plant matter. You can also experiment. Offer a dish with a variety of finely chopped vegetables or fruits, and observe which ones the animal seems to prefer. Good choices are:

Banana (small amounts)
Chopped apple
Finely chopped green beans
Finely chopped mixed vegetables (fresh or frozen and thawed)
Grated carrots
Grated squash
Leafy greens such as kale, romaine lettuce, mustard and collard greens
Peach
Peas

Day geckos (*Phelsuma*), prehensile-tailed geckos (*Rhacodactylus*), Madagascar velvet geckos (*Homopholis*), and others will readily accept banana or peach baby food with a little calcium carbonate mixed in. You can try this with other geckos or lizards and observe their responses.

Commercial Lizard Diets
In recent years, various commercial diets for omnivorous and frugivorous lizards have become available. These have proved useful as a primary or supplemental diet.

Some gecko species enjoy lapping up fruit-flavored baby food.

Currently, complete dry diets for iguanas and bearded dragons (also usable with *Uromastyx*) are sold. However, none are ideal if used as an exclusive diet, and some may cause health problems if an adequate source of water is not provided. In addition, some individuals will not readily eat these diets without some work to entice them, such as initially mixing the diet with a preferred food. These diets are probably best considered as a component of a varied diet.

Exceptions include the T-Rex Superfoods diets for *Rhacodactylus* geckos. These have been extensively tested on large captive populations and proved excellent as a primary diet for the maintenance and breeding of those species as well as for other fruit-eating lizards. Zoo Med has a powdered day gecko food that can be eaten dry and that supplements an insect diet, providing vitamins and minerals. Species with omnivorous tendencies will also lick and ingest some of these gecko diets, including anole species, a number of skinks, some lacertids and plated lizards, and others.

Meat

Many lizards that are frequent tongue flickers will feed on nonmoving food items. Fine strips of lean beef (such as flank steak) or beef heart and cooked chicken will be taken by these species. They should be supplemented with a calcium-vitamin D_3 supplement. For lizards that will eat them, these foods can make up one component of a varied diet. Until

A Sample Gut-Loading Diet for Insects	
Fresh Foods (Twice per Week)	**Grains and Seeds (Once per Week)**
Kale	Baby cereal flakes
Mustard greens	Ground rodent chow
Collard greens	Ground oatmeal
Carrots	Ground barley
Green beans	Sesame seeds (small amount)
Grated squashes	(high calcium/high fat)
Orange slices	

Note: Add finely powdered calcium carbonate to the above foods.

research demonstrates differently, they should not make up more than one-fourth of the animal's diet.

Water

All insect-eating lizards should be provided with some water. As a rule, terrestrial lizards readily drink out of a shallow water container. The height of the water container is important. It should be shallow enough for a terrestrial lizard to see over the rim when in an active position, raised on its four legs. Finding suitable containers may take a little effort. For miniature species, use plastic bottle caps or the clear plastic casters (for placing under furniture legs) sold in hardware stores. Import stores offer a variety of small containers that may prove invaluable, from ashtrays to sushi dipping containers. Avoid jar lids that can become corroded. For larger species, ashtrays, plastic food storage containers, and pet water bowls work well. Plastic ice cream container tops make excellent dishes for smaller terrestrial lizards.

A number of arboreal lizards drink readily only from droplets of water. The reflection of light against the droplets seems to play a key role in terms of these species recognizing water. Anoles and true chameleons are the best known examples of this type of lizard. Even the arboreal lizards that do drink water from a container will drink more readily from droplets. Many of the geckos, including day geckos, tend to be droplet drinkers.

Misting is the primary method used by herpetoculturists for providing water to arboreal species that drink readily only from droplets. You can also place a container with a pinhole in the underside above the vivarium. Another shallow container is placed on the floor of the vivarium. Water is placed in the top container and allowed to drip onto the leaves of plants that have been carefully placed above the lower container where the dripping water eventually collects. The lizards are drawn to the water because it is in motion and reflects light. An alternative used by some chameleon keepers is an intravenous drip, such as those used in hospitals. The unit is placed above the vivarium, filled with purified water, and the drip rate regulated. Here again, a shallow container is placed at the bottom of the vivarium to collect the water.

In most cases, tap water is adequate for insect-eating lizards. However, many herpetoculturists want to eliminate any possible negative effects of tap water and thus select bottled water for drinking and purified water, which is very low in minerals and other dissolved substances, when misting. Misting with purified water is less likely to leave mineral deposits on the glass. High quality of water is important to the health of your animals.

CHAPTER 16

HANDLING

Most lizards should be kept in vivaria in which they can be observed. As is true with keeping tropical fish, the animals' appearance, aesthetics, and behaviors are the primary sources of enjoyment to be derived from keeping them. Handling should be a secondary activity only.

Many lizards are quite fast and tend to scurry when given the opportunity. However, some of the medium-to-large species, which tend to be relatively calm and not subject to sudden panic or flight behaviors, are suitable for handling or as pets. Among these are some of the terrestrial geckos, including the popular leopard geckos and fat-tail geckos. Other geckos, such as prehensile-tailed geckos (*Rhacodactylus*), can also be handled for short periods of time. Australian dragons of the genus *Pogona* are very docile and among the best lizard pets one can own. Calm when handled, they are even recommended for children as

Few lizards relish being handled. Avoid handling your lizard excessively.

long as there is some adult supervision. Plated lizards, particularly *Gerrhosaurus major*, can also be handled. Some very tame plated lizards can even be carried on the shoulders of their owners. Some of the larger skinks, such as Schneider's skinks (*Eumeces schneideri*), anguids, as well as larger lacertas such as the green lacerta (*Lacerta viridis*) also tolerate some handling. As a rule, larger lizards, which are not prone to panic or flight behaviors, are the best lizards for handling. Observation and experimentation will aid in determining the degree to which a lizard can be handled. If having a lizard that is an easily handled pet is a primary goal for you, consider some of the species mentioned, particularly the inland bearded dragon (*Pogona vitticeps*).

Regardless of a species' amenability to handling, no hatchling or juvenile lizards should be handled when they are small. Immature lizards are much more prone to flight behaviors and are often more delicate than adults. Although adult bearded dragons are highly recommended for handling, young dragons are somewhat delicate and should not be handled while they are small. When they are small, leopard geckos can be feisty and prone to sudden dashes, seldom remaining calm in the hand. In contrast, with regular handling, many of the adults make relatively nice pets.

When experimenting with handling a species, always do so in a room with little furniture and the door kept shut.

Be careful not to drop a fidgety lizard.

Make sure there are no open areas allowing for escape outside or furniture that can be climbed into or under. Escapes under and into the mechanism of a stove or refrigerator could present a serious problem. Handle lizards on or over a table, rather than in the middle of the room. A table will minimize the distance a lizard falls if it should escape your grasp during handling.

CHAPTER 17

DISEASES AND DISORDERS

Insect-eating lizards, being for the most part of small to moderate size, are generally more difficult to treat than are larger vertebrate-eating or vegetarian lizards. For this reason, the importance of disease prevention cannot be overemphasized.

The following are essential guidelines for disease prevention:

Carefully select animals prior to purchase. Avoid thin, listless, or sick-looking animals. If several specimens in a given group of imported animals appear ill, even the healthy-appearing animals may have been infected with various disease organisms by other members of the group. Do not buy a lizard from such a group.

Unfortunately, there may be times in your animal's life when it must visit a veterinarian.

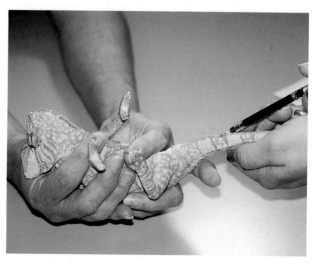

Substandard environmental factors, such as temperature, humidity, substrate type, and landscaping, can provide conditions that lead to disease. Social stress factors, such as bullying by conspecifics and competition for food or vivarium niches, can also be important factors leading to susceptibility to disease-causing organisms. Always evaluate environmental and social conditions when an animal appears sick. Make necessary changes to rectify problem situations.

Whenever possible, purchase captive-bred or -raised animals; they are less likely to be parasitized or diseased.

Quarantine all new animals for at least thirty (preferably sixty to ninety) days prior to introducing them into a vivarium with other lizards. If possible, quarantine them in a separate room. Adopt maintenance procedures to help prevent infection of healthy animals. Healthy animals should be cared for first, followed by potentially healthy animals in quarantine. Sick animals should always be maintained last. At the end of the maintenance schedule, wash thoroughly with a disinfectant such as Betadine scrub, and avoid contact with healthy animals the remainder of that day. Any tools should be disinfected after each use and a different set of tools used with each respective group of animals. Many people ignore the quarantining of animals and later deeply regret this when most of their collection becomes ill and is wiped out. *Please heed this advice.*

Deparasitize animals. Internal parasites play an important role in the inability of imported animals to establish to captivity. Many imported insect-eating lizards harbor nematodes, tapeworms, or flagellate protozoa. However, because many insect-eating lizards are small, treating them for parasites (in terms of dosages and administration) can present challenges. As a rule, the easiest way to administer medications is orally. With very large groups of very small lizards, it is sometimes best to weigh the entire group, finely pulverize the appropriate amount of medication with a mortar and pestle, and use the crushed medication as a powder to coat food insects. Place the insects in a container with the pulverized medication,

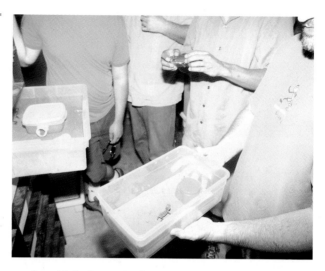

The best way to avoid unhealthy animals is to carefully examine lizards before buying them.

gently swirl the insects in the mix, and offer the coated insects to the lizards. The dosage will be variable and inaccurate, but this method is sometimes the best recourse for treating large groups of inexpensive lizards. Fenbendazole (Panacur) in liquid form, appropriately diluted, can easily be administered to small species with an eyedropper (see Klingenberg 2007).

Having an accurate weighing instrument that measures in fine increments (such as a triple beam or digital scale) and knowing how to properly dissolve medication and determine dosage are essential for treating individual lizards. Because of miscalculation, inexperienced herpetoculturists sometimes administer up to ten times the recommended dose of a medication. In terms of parasite treatment, because many small insect-eating lizards are relatively inexpensive, the veterinary cost of treating them or checking them for parasites can exceed many times the initial cost of the lizards. Furthermore, having spent all that money, there is no guarantee that the lizards will survive.

Keep animals in properly designed vivaria that meet their essential requirements. Inadequate environments can significantly stress animals and contribute to their decline and susceptibility to disease. Inappropriate or inadequate temperature, relative humidity, water availability, landscaping, and social conditions are all factors that can contribute to stress and to failure of an animal to adapt to captivity. It is important to maintain setups on a regular basis and to provide a high-quality diet, along with high-quality water.

Monitor animals daily and visually check them to discern their health status. Always segregate and quarantine any animals that appear ill or stressed as soon as they are noticed.

Veterinarians

Generally, insect-eating lizards that appear very sick do not survive, even if you take them to a veterinarian. Like birds, lizards often do not display obvious symptoms until they are very ill. The earliest symptoms tend to be so subtle that you may not notice them or may just think the animal is having a bad day. Unfortunately, the next step can be a very sudden decline, from "Sherman's not feeling very peppy today" to "Sherman's lying on the bottom of his cage, barely moving." At this stage, you may panic and call for an appointment with a veterinarian, hoping for a miracle. In most cases, the miracle doesn't happen. Sherman checks out and ends up with the winged lizards in saurian heaven. You end up $35 poorer and disappointed in the veterinarian who couldn't save your lizard.

There are better ways to make a decision about taking your lizard to the veterinarian:

Locate an experienced reptile veterinarian before you need one. Good sources of information for reptile veterinarians

Shown is an example of a quarantine cage.

in your area are herpetological societies, herpetoculturists (particularly commercial breeders), and reptile dealers. Another option is to look in the telephone directory and find a veterinarian who advertises that he or she is experienced with reptiles or exotic animals.

Consult a veterinarian soon after purchase, when the animal is healthy. Prevention is always the best course with reptiles. If you have just purchased a relatively valuable lizard, such as a Parson's chameleon, a green tree monitor, or an adult double-crested basilisk, you will want to know whether the animal is healthy and whether it harbors parasites. In this situation, consult a reptile veterinarian and have a general examination plus a fecal exam performed. Green tree monitors, for example, are imported and often arrive with protozoan infections. Untreated, these animals will decline and eventually die. Treated, they will often thrive and live for many years.

In the case of small and inexpensive lizards, you may need to carefully weigh financial considerations. The cost of a veterinary visit and parasite check can amount to several times the cost of the animal. If you are careful in your selection, there is a good chance that your animal will be relatively healthy. The decision is up to you.

If one of your lizards appears ill but still has some vigor, waste no time in taking it to a qualified veterinarian. Early diagnosis and treatment are critical if it is to survive. When you bring your animal to a veterinarian, be candid about what you can or cannot spend. This allows a veterinarian to provide you with options for treatment. For example, a veterinarian may say that she suspects that your animal has X parasites, and that tests to determine this will cost X amount. She may suggest that instead of administering the tests, the lizard's treatment be based on assumption and then confirmed with improvement. In other cases, the veterinarian may state that the cost of treatment would be very prohibitive and not necessarily succeed, so it might be better to euthanize the animal or let the disease follow its course. Ultimately, the decision as to what to do and what you can afford is yours alone.

If your lizard is small, common, relatively inexpensive, and is looking very ill (listless, eyes are closed or barely open, and very thin), resign yourself to the fact that your lizard is unlikely to survive. The cost of veterinary treatment will ultimately be much higher than it is to replace the lizard, and the animal is probably going to die no matter what you do. When small lizards go downhill, they quickly (even within a few days' time) reach a point of no return. Save yourself the money, the energy, and the grief. If you have a good rapport with a reptile veterinarian, she will probably give you the same advice or charge you a minimal fee for a quick prognosis. If you have a valuable animal or an animal that you dearly care for, the animal still has a little spunk, and you can afford to spend the money (knowing that it may well be of no use), then you may want to consult with an experienced reptile veterinarian.

Veterinarians are often quite effective in treating a lizard that has injured itself but otherwise appears quite healthy. Again, cost is a key factor.

Common Health Problems for Insect-Eating Lizards

Following are discussions of a number of diseases and other health problems commonly found in insect-eating lizards, along with treatment options.

External Parasites

Wild-collected imported lizards can sometimes carry external parasites. They should always be examined closely and treated as needed.

Ticks

Some species of wild-collected insect-eating lizards harbor ticks. These external parasites can be seen as flat scalelike creatures, either imbedded between scales or embedded in the soft skin of armpits, groins, or eyelids. Because they suck the blood of lizards and can transmit diseases, they should always be removed when noticed. Tweezers should be used to remove individual ticks. Using a cotton swab

dipped in rubbing alcohol, apply it to the body of the tick, and then wait five to ten minutes before tweezing. Some imported true chameleons harbor such large numbers of small ticks in the armpits that removing all the ticks at one time could cause trauma. In these cases, rubbing alcohol is applied to all tick bodies, but they are removed a few at a time over a period of several days.

Mites

These small beadlike parasites are not common in fine-scaled insect-eating lizards or burrowing insect-eating lizards. They are seen on some of the larger skinks and on species with large overlapping scales, such as swifts (*Sceloporus*). The presence of white flecks (mite feces) on the skin of an animal is a reliable indicator of mite infestation. Examining an animal with a magnifying glass or running a moist paper towel across the skin of a lizard (then checking the towel visually) are two other methods to determine the presence of mites.

The treatment of mites in insect-eating lizards can be difficult. If seen on a lizard with fine-grained skin, such as a day gecko (usually infested by mites from other lizard species kept in dealers' facilities), the best solution is to thoroughly wash or spray the animal with water (in a location where the mites can be flushed down a sink) until it is clear of mites. Then, keep the animal in a relatively bare enclosure for at least three weeks until you are sure all mites are gone. Relatively few mites will live and breed on insect-eating lizards with fine, nonoverlapping scales. With some desert lizards, particularly species that burrow, keeping them on a fine silica sand substrate will result in a gradual decrease and eventual elimination of mites.

Some species, such as certain swifts, can harbor difficult-to-eradicate species of mites. One method of killing these mites consists of placing a vapona pest strip (No-Pest). Place a ½-inch by 3-inch (12.7- by 76.2-mm) pest strip impregnated with 2.2 dichlorovinyl dimethyl phosphate in a small plastic container with perforations (such as a deli cup), and then put the container into the enclosure. The enclosure should be at least 30 gallons and should be partially covered, with an opening left to allow for some air flow. Mites will usually be killed within twelve hours. (Note: Some lizards may be sensitive to pest strips; use alternative treatments).

The animal(s) should then be removed from the existing enclosure. Thoroughly wash and disinfect the enclosure with a 5 percent bleach solution. Dispose of or wash all landscape materials with a 5 percent bleach solution. The lizards can then be placed back into a newly designed setup. Reptile mites usually lay their eggs in the areas surrounding their host, rather than on the host. Monitor the animal carefully, and repeat treatment if the animal becomes reinfected. An alternative treatment that has proven safe and effective with most lizards (but not skinks) is the use of ivermectin in a spray form (0.5 mL of Ivomec, 10 percent solution in a quart of water). Frontline dog flea spray has also proved very effective (usually one spray, avoiding the eyes), but not enough information is available as to its safety with various lizard species. I have safely used a single spray to treat mites in giant geckos (*Rhacodactylus leachianus*) and gargoyle geckos (*Rhacodactylus auriculatus*).

If you want to treat your lizards on your own, it is critical that you research any information on the subject available in books or on the Internet. It is best to consult an experienced reptile veterinarian. Fortunately, most of the insect-eating lizards sold in the pet trade do not usually harbor mites.

Internal Parasites

As a rule, all wild-collected animals are infested with internal parasites. Parasites with direct life cycles (such as pinworms and hookworms) can, under captive conditions, increase to life-threatening levels; they should be treated. Certain species of insect-eating lizards, such as some of the true chameleons, are infested with such large numbers of nematodes that captive stress quickly leads to an imbalance between parasite and host. For this reason, many herpetoculturists treat any new animals with fenbendazole (Panacur) at a dosage of 50 mg/kg (repeat weekly for up to three doses). Insect-eating lizards can also have parasites for which they are not the primary host but are an intermediate host.

Some of these parasites will eventually burrow through the host and get lodged underneath the skin or sometimes in the lungs. Some of the filarial nematodes and plerocercoid tapeworms fall into this category. Some wild-collected

Coccidia and pinworms were found in a bearded dragon.

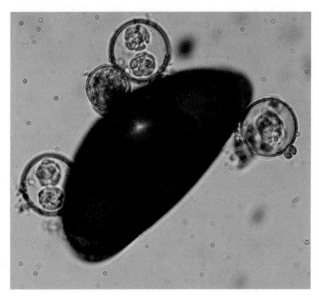

These nematode parasites were from a bearded dragon.

lizards, notably chameleons, can have high loads of filarial worms (similar to heartworm) that end up lodged under the skin and need to be surgically removed.

Many imported lizards from tropical areas may be infected with flagellate protozoa because of the filthy conditions in which they are maintained in dealers' compounds. Routine treatment with metronidazole (Flagyl) at 50 mg/kg has proved beneficial for many of these species. For more information on parasites and parasite treatment, see Klingenberg (2007, a work geared to herpetoculturists) and Mader (2006).

Skin Diseases and Shedding Problems

A variety of skin diseases are found among insect-eating lizards; they range from bacterial infections to certain skin cancers. Many skin diseases are associated with improper environmental conditions (such as too much moisture, which can lead to bacterial or fungal infections). Others, including certain types of cancers, are transmitted from other animals. Fortunately, most insect-eating lizards are not prone to skin diseases (see Mader 2006 for more information).

Improper environmental conditions are the primary cause of shedding problems in insect-eating lizards; they

A sailfin lizard eats shedding skin on its foot.

are usually inadequate in terms of relative humidity, substrate, or landscaping. For example, many geckos, including terrestrial species, will shed more easily if relative humidity is 50 percent or more. In the wild, the relative humidity in shelters is consistently higher than in the open. Another cause of shedding problems is illness. Sick lizards are often too weak to adequately perform shedding behavior and may manifest shedding problems. In those cases, if the skin is loose and lifting from the body, you can assist the lizard by manually removing the shed. The cause of illness should be diagnosed and the lizard treated. Unusually, frequent shedding is also associated with illness.

In captivity, another cause of shedding problems in species with a low tolerance to excessive vitamin A levels is hypervitaminosis A. Some of the day geckos, including *Phelsuma standingi,* fat-tail geckos (*Hemitheconyx caudicinctus*), and some true chameleons (e.g., *C. pardalis* and *C. johnstoni*) are sensitive vitamin A. Switching to supplements with a low vitamin A content will usually reverse the situation.

Metabolic Bone Disease and Calcium Deficiency

Symptoms of calcium deficiency were common among insect-eating lizards before the use of vitamin-mineral supplementation of food insects. Fast-growing hatchlings, newborns, and breeding females are particularly susceptible. With proper husbandry, this disease is easily prevented. In insect-eating lizards, metabolic bone disease and calcium deficiency are caused by the following:

- Lack of calcium in the diet
- Lack of vitamin D_3, which is necessary for calcium to be absorbed
- Inadequate calcium-to-phosphorus ratio. The ratio of calcium to phosphorus in the diet of lizards should be two parts calcium to one part phosphorus (2:1).
- Unavailability of natural sunlight to allow an animal to synthesize its own vitamin D_3. In captivity, this is usually remedied more or less effectively by providing vitamin D_3 orally through food-insect supplementation. An alternative is the use of UVB-generating bulbs.
- Excessive amounts of vitamin A in some species

Shed boxes can help raise the humidity level, which often helps alleviate shedding problems.

Symptoms of calcium deficiency and metabolic bone disease include:

- Flexible lower jaw, skull bones, or limbs; foreshortening of the lower jaw
- Deformities of the jaws, backbone, and tail
- Inability to feed
- Hind limb paralysis; listlessness
- Fibrous osteodystrophy resulting in swollen appearance of jaws or limbs
- Decalcified eggs in gravid females

Treatment includes daily oral administration of calcium and vitamin D_3 supplements, plus brief (three to four hours daily), regular exposure to sunlight or to an artificial UVB source (mercury vapor UVB bulbs are very effective). In severe cases, a veterinarian can administer injectable calcium.

Injuries

Minor injuries, including skin lacerations, should be cleaned with a disinfectant solution (Betadine) followed by application of an antibiotic ointment such as Neosporin. Deep injuries, including lacerations that do not close, deep bites, or puncture wounds, require similar treatment. They may

This veiled chameleon has metabolic bone disease.

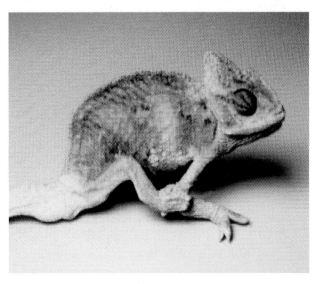

This bearded dragon has a bite wound on its leg.

also require stitches and injectable antibiotics. A reptile veterinarian is best qualified to perform such procedures. Any injured animal should be removed from the conditions, either physical or social, that led to the trauma. Keep the animal on a simple and relatively sterile substrate, such as newsprint or brown butcher paper, while recovering.

Swellings and Lumps

Lizards may develop swollen areas—commonly toes, but jaws, limbs, and the cloacal area can also be affected. These swellings are often due to infections that will have to be incised, emptied, flushed, and treated with antibiotics. In some cases, lumps will turn out to be tumors.

Consult a qualified veterinarian in most cases. Filthy and overcrowded conditions increase the probability of infections, so correcting environmental conditions is very important.

Respiratory Infections

In smaller lizards, the most obvious symptoms of respiratory infection are labored breathing, gaping, forced exhalations, inactivity, and failure to feed. If the lizard is held while you use the end of your thumb to gently press up against the throat, mucus may be seen emerging through the nostrils. In the earliest stages, raising the temperature to 88°F to 90°F may allow the animal's immune system to overcome the infection. In serious cases, an antibiotic must be administered; however, antibiotic treatment of a small lizard may prove difficult. A reptile veterinarian should be consulted. Be aware that the smaller the lizard, the quicker its rate of decline, and the smaller the chance that veterinary treatment will be successful.

Sudden Weight Loss in Imported Lizards
The sudden decline usually associated with weight loss in imported lizards is often caused by internal parasites having a

A healthy leopard gecko has a fat tail (right). A less-healthy leopard gecko (left) shows signs of emaciation.

Keep close track of your lizard's stools to ensure that it isn't suffering from gastrointestinal problems.

negative impact on the host, following exposure to prolonged stress (usually environmental). Rehydrate the animal twice daily by administering electrolytes orally with an eye dropper (Gatorade or infant electrolytes such as Pedialyte). Have the animal checked for internal parasites and treated as needed. Inadequate environmental conditions, viral diseases, and social stress can also lead to failure to feed and sudden weight loss.

Gastroenteritis

Infections of the GI tract are common in imported lizards. Symptoms of gastroenteritis include runny or discolored stools, bloody stools, and unusually smelly stools. These symptoms are usually accompanied by weight loss, listlessness, and loss of appetite. The recommended course of treatment is to have a fecal exam performed by a veterinarian and to treat the animal accordingly. Flagellate protozoa are a common cause of gastroenteritis in imported lizards. These are easily treated with metronidazole (Flagyl) at a dose of 50 mg/kg, administered orally, and repeated in four days. Coccidia and *Pseudomonas* are two other common causes of gastroenteritis in captive lizards.

Salmonellosis

Salmonellosis is a disease caused by the bacteria of the genus *Salmonella*. This disease can be transmitted from infected animals to humans. In humans, it causes nausea, vomiting, and diarrhea; in severe cases, it can cause paralysis, coma, and (rarely) death. Young children, immunosuppressed adults, and older people can die if infected with *Salmonella*. Some cases that have attracted great attention are associated with green iguanas. If you consider the number of these animals imported each year (hundreds of thousands), the number of people infected has been relatively very small.

To prevent any problems with *Salmonella*, adopt the following guidelines:

- Do not allow children to handle lizards without supervision. Teach them to not put their hands in their mouths when handling lizards. Always wash hands after handling lizards, preferably with a bactericidal soap.
- Do not practice lizard maintenance procedures in areas, or with utensils, used by humans. This includes not cleaning out enclosures in the kitchen, not allowing animals on kitchen counters or in sinks or bathtubs, and not using human food utensils for animal maintenance. If there is crossover, all areas and utensils should be washed and disinfected after each exposure.
- If your animal shows symptoms associated with salmonellosis (listlessness, loss of appetite, weight loss, and wet, loose stools), have a veterinarian perform a fecal exam. If infected, one course is to euthanize the animal; another is to attempt treatment. Failure to notice symptoms of salmonellosis does not mean that your animal is not infected because many reptiles can be symptomless carriers. If you are concerned about your children or immunosuppressed individuals, have fecal exams performed as a routine procedure.

In conclusion, salmonellosis contracted from insect-eating lizards is very rare. Even people in the pet industry, handling thousands of lizards per year, are rarely infected. The few cases of salmonellosis contracted by humans from lizards are associated primarily with green iguanas. With a minimum of common sense (such as washing hands after handling), there is very little risk of contracting *Salmonella* from lizards. You probably have a greater risk of contracting *Salmonella* from poorly cooked eggs or chicken than from lizards.

Egg Binding

Gravid female lizards, particularly imported species, can suffer from egg binding, also known as egg retention. There are various causes of egg binding in lizards. One common cause is the absence of a suitable environment for the laying of eggs. To provide a good egg-laying environment, try one of the following methods: provide a shelter over a container of moist medium; add freshly dug soil to the enclosure, and dig a preliminary burrow entrance for your lizard; lay a slab of wood over a portion of moist substratum; place vertical egg-laying sites in the enclosure, such as hollow bamboo stems. For egg-bound females that are off feed but still appear healthy, give a protein supplement such as Ensure (available in drugstores) plus calcium with a feeding syringe once or twice daily.

As soon as females seem to become even slightly weakened and listless, contact your veterinarian. The usual veterinary procedure involves taking an X-ray to assess the condition of the female. On the basis of the evaluation, a veterinarian may recommend administering calcium, possibly giving a hormone that induces contractions, or surgical removal of eggs. If an animal dies, the eggs can sometimes be saved if surgically removed soon after death (preferably within a few minutes).

Cloacal Prolapse

Parasite infection, enteric disease, or, in some cases, accumulation of fecal material that contains large chitinous parts can cause an eversion of the cloaca (terminal intestinal tract). If noticed early, the everted section can be gently reinserted (reverted) into place using a moistened cotton swab. If not noticed within hours of occurrence, the everted section will swell, become damaged, and eventually dry out or become infected. With valuable lizards, immediate attention by a qualified veterinarian is recommended.

Hemipenile Prolapse

With male lizards, a hemipenis may fail to retract following eversion. If not reverted inside the base of the tail, the hemipenis will swell, become damaged and dried, and eventually be lost. Depending on conditions, a secondary infection may develop. With larger lizards, you can try to carefully and gently revert a recently everted hemipenis using a moistened cotton swab; or immediately make an appointment with a veterinarian.

CHAPTER 18

SHIPPING AND RECEIVING

Mail order makes up a significant portion of the reptile trade. Thousands of lizards are shipped every year across the United States and in some cases abroad. If you are going to ship reptiles, there are two important things you must do: make sure that any required paperwork is taken care of, and verify the legalities of shipping the animals. For example, in some states, permits may be required to own certain lizards, and in California, lizards cannot be legally collected and sold for commercial purposes.

A number of states require health certificates for shipping or receiving reptiles. As I have indicated at various hearings, the certificates are often signed off without inspection by veterinarians. At best, a quick visual inspection could reveal obvious disease but very likely would fail to detect a

This is the proper way to ship a group of small lizards.

contagious or dangerous one. A thin import can be misdiagnosed as ill and vice versa—healthy-appearing animals carrying, say, cryptosporidiosis, coccidiosis, or a deadly virus may be labeled as healthy. Members of the pet trade will not tolerate shipments of obviously sick animals for very long, and the issue is essentially self-correcting.

Most lizard diseases are not zoonotic. The most common one, salmonellosis, will not be identified by inspection and is simply best prevented by common sense hygiene.

How to Ship

Lizards in the United States are shipped primarily by air freight or by various forms of overnight mail. At this time, lizards can be shipped by United States Postal Service Express Mail, FedEx, United Parcel Service, and DHL overnight shipping. Ship reptiles only during times of the year when temperatures are mild, neither too cold (40°F or above) nor too hot (88°F or under). Check weather reports for the areas of departure and destination when you ship animals. Never ship lizards during unusually cold periods or during heat waves.

Call the shipping company to determine whether it provides overnight service to your intended receiving area. If shipping by air, ask the air freight office whether the particular airline you have in mind will transport live lizards, what flight your animal(s) should be on, and at what time you should be at the airport (typically the airlines recommend that you be there about two hours before flight time).

It is a good idea to insure animals for their full value when shipping, particularly if they are valuable. Unfortunately, airlines do occasionally lose shipments. Notify the person receiving the animals by telephone or e-mail, providing a tracking number and the time you shipped the animals and their estimated time of arrival. Ask that you be notified if the animals do not arrive as expected.

Packing for Shipment

Lizards should be shipped in a polystyrene foam shipping container with a cardboard box exterior. You may have to contact tropical fish stores to obtain these containers. You can also make a polystyrene foam-lined cardboard box. Just buy an insulation foam panel at a large hardware store. Use a utility knife to cut the panels, and tape them together with duct tape inside a cardboard box.

Use a knife or a screwdriver to poke one hole through each side of the box, making sure it goes through both the cardboard and polystyrene foam liner. The holes are required for adequate ventilation. As should be obvious, be sure to make the holes before introducing the animals into the box.

The lizards, depending on size, should be placed in perforated (air holes) plastic deli cups, perforated plastic food containers, cloth bags, or in cardboard containers such as milk cartons. Add some shredded newspaper or paper toweling to the bag or container because the lizard may be bounced around during transport. Make sure you punch or drill holes in the container or cartons for ventilation. Cloth bags can be sealed with tape or the ends tied in a knot or fastened with rubber bands (be careful of the lizards). Milk cartons can be stapled or taped. Cardboard boxes can be taped. Next, place the bag(s) or containers in the shipping

This large lizard was improperly shipped in a cloth sack that was too small.

box, and use crumpled newspaper to prevent shifting during the journey.

During cool weather, chemical heat packs can be used to keep the lizards warm. Tape the packs to the inside of the polystyrene shipping box, either to the top or sides. Heat packs should not have direct contact with either bags or cardboard boxes because of the possible risk of overheating. During unusually warm weather, cool packs can be used, placed in such a way that they are not in contact with the inside containers. Some herpetoculturists place them in cardboard boxes or in plastic containers with multiple holes punched in them.

You are now ready to seal the shipping box. Many herpetoculturists place an invoice or care instructions inside the box at this point. Others tape them in an envelope to the outside. Tape any required paperwork to the outside of the shipping box. Close the box and seal with packing tape or duct tape. Make sure that the ventilation holes are not covered. Label the box, indicating who it is being shipped to and the shipper. Always include the phone numbers of both persons. On top of the box, indicate the number of animals included in the box and the genus and species of the animals. Write Harmless Lizards on the top of the box in large lettering. On the sides, write This Side Up, with arrows pointing to the top of the box. On both the sides and on the top of the box, write Keep at 70°F to 80°F and Live Lizards.

Receiving Animals

When receiving animals by air, carefully open up the shipment at the airport to verify the state of the animals if there has been a problem or delay with the shipment. Do this

Laws

Check state, local, and federal laws before collecting, receiving, or shipping U.S. species. If shipping to another country, check CITES (Convention on International Trade in Endangered Species) regulations and the Endangered Species Act. Write or call United States Fish and Wildlife for necessary information.

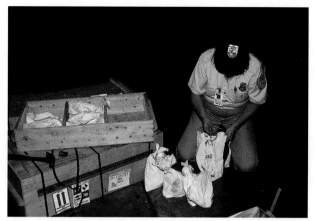

A U.S. Fish and Wildlife officer inspects a shipment of lizards.

very carefully to prevent any possibility of escape; you simply want to ascertain whether the animals are alive. If the animals arrive dead, this can be verified by airline employees and a claim form filed. This procedure can facilitate your being compensated by the shipper. Airlines will often replace the animals for their invoiced or insured value plus air freight costs if it can be determined that the death of the animals was due to the airline's negligence (e.g., a shipment gets lost for several days during cold weather).

Do not open animal shipments inside a post office. Commercial shippers do not guarantee live arrivals. Instead, open the package at home, and have a digital camera ready to record any dead or sick animals. Notify the seller or shipper immediately if you hope to receive a credit or refund.

CHAPTER 19

GENERAL GUIDELINES FOR POPULAR INSECT-EATING LIZARDS

T hese are very general guidelines for the herpetoculture of some of the more popular insect-eating lizard species. For more information about the lizard species you intend to keep, purchase all the available literature that addresses its needs.

Eublepharidae (Geckos with Movable Eyelids)

The eublepharids are geckos that have movable eyelids and lack pads of lamellae at the ends of their digits (the sticky ridges that allow some geckos to walk on vertical surfaces). They are all terrestrial with the exception of *Aeluroscalabotes*, which is semi-arboreal. As a broad rule (there are many exceptions), geckos are among the easiest to keep of the lizards. Males have hemipenile bulges and enlarged preanal pores. Eublepharids include the leopard geckos (*Eublepharis*), Asian leopard geckos of the genus *Goniurosaurus*, fat-tail geckos (*Hemitheconyx*), the bare-toed gecko (*Holodactylus*), banded geckos (*Coleonyx*), and the cat gecko (*Aeluroscalabotes*).

The leopard gecko (*Eublepharis macularius)* and the African fat-tail gecko (*Hemitheconyx caudicinctus*) are the most readily available of the eublepharids. They can be maintained in desert vivaria with both dry and humidified shelters. A damp sand or soil area should be available for egg laying. African fat-tail geckos have also been successfully maintained on orchid bark. Daytime temperatures should be in the low 80s F (26.7°C to 28.3°C), and nighttime temperatures can drop into the 70s F (21°C to 26°C). Leopard geckos will tolerate nighttime temperatures in the 60s F (15.6°C to 20.6°C) during the winter. A slight winter drop in temperature of 5 to 7 degrees F (2.8 to 3.9 degrees C), along with a photoperiod reduction, is recommended for fat-tail geckos. Breeding groups should consist of one male with several females. Both species will breed readily and lay several clutches of two eggs each year.

North American desert banded geckos (*Coleonyx*) can be kept under conditions similar to leopard geckos, but their diet will have to be adjusted to their small size. Winter cooling is recommended for breeding the desert *Coleonyx*. Tropical *Coleonyx* should be kept in tropical vivaria on orchid bark or a potting soil and orchid bark mix. They should be kept at temperatures in the high 70s to low 80s F (25°C to 28.3°C). A moist substrate should be available for egg laying. The attractive Central American banded gecko (*Coleonyx mitratus*) is now being bred in increasing numbers in the United States. The cat gecko (*Aeluroscalabotes felinus*) can be kept under similar conditions as tropical

Quarantine all lizards, including captive-bred leopard geckos, to prevent spreading any disease to an existing collection.

Coleonyx, but it is critical that relative humidity be around 80 percent.

In recent years, Chinese eublepharids of the genus *Goniurosaurus* have become established. They can be treated like tropical *Coleonyx*, with a maximum daytime temperature of 80°F, the upper 70s being preferable. The Japanese *Goniurosaurus* will not tolerate high temperatures and is best maintained in the mid- to high 70s F during the daytime, with slight drops at night.

Shown is a "white line" fat tail gecko (*Hemitheconyx caudicinctus*).

Gekkonidae (Geckos with Immovable Eyelids)

Like eublepharidae, gekkonidae are among the easiest to keep of the pet lizards. Some of the gekkonidae include the day geckos (*Phelsuma*) and frog-eyed geckos (*Teratoscincus*). Frog-eyed geckos (*Teratoscincus*) can be maintained as leopard geckos are, although they do appreciate an opportunity to bask, particularly at the end of the day. Make a low-wattage red light and basking area available for their use. Some herpetoculturists supply frog-eyed geckos with a black light because it may be beneficial for successful breeding. Breeding success depends on calcium availability, along with temperatures into the low 60s F (15.6°C to 20.6°C) at night and a reduced winter photoperiod. These are some of

The lined day gecko (*Phelsuma lineata bombetokensis*) is considered a good gecko for beginners.

the most beautiful of the terrestrial geckos (particularly *T. keyserlingii)*, and efforts should be made to breed them more consistently. *Gekko* (*G. gekko, G. vittatus,* etc.), house geckos, and flying geckos (*Ptychozoon*) should be kept in tropical vivaria. They are generally easy to keep and breed. Imports should be checked and treated for internal parasites. Most male geckos have pronounced hemipenile bulges. In many species, males also have enlarged preanal or femoral pores.

Bent-toed geckos (*Cyrtodactylus*) are generally considered somewhat difficult. They should be kept in tropical vivaria with moderate to high relative humidity. Orchid bark is an adequate substrate; so is a peat moss-based potting soil. Provide shelters as well as climbing areas. Temperatures should be moderate (in the mid-70s to low 80s F (23.3°C to 28.3°C) during the day and in the low to mid-70s F (21°C to 26°C) at night. Imports should be treated for internal parasites. Once established, certain species, such as *Cyrtodactylus pulchellus,* can be quite hardy. More efforts should be made to establish these species in captivity.

Day geckos (*Phelsuma*) are now imported in large numbers from Madagascar. They are some of the jewels of the lizard world. Many of the species are very hardy, adaptable,

Day geckos, such as this Mauritius day gecko (*Phelsuma cepediana*), are considered the jewels of the lizard world by some.

and among the easiest to keep of the lizards. The giant day gecko (*Phelsuma madagascariensis grandis*) and several of the dwarf day geckos (*Phelsuma laticauda, Phelsuma lineata, Phelsuma quadriocellata, Phelsuma serraticauda*) are recommended for beginners. Most of these lizards will fare well in planted tropical vivaria at temperatures in the high 70s to mid-80s F (25°C to 28.3°C). They are primarily insect eaters but also relish soft fruit and fruit baby foods. Provide water through misting. Many species are easy to breed. See McKeown (1993) for details on their herpetoculture. Most species should be kept in single pairs; others can be kept in small colonies in large vivaria. Females lay several clutches of two eggs each year.

Madagascar velvet geckos (*Homopholis*) can be kept and bred under conditions similar to those required by day geckos. They should be kept in single pairs. Moorish and white-spotted geckos (*Tarentola mauritanica, Tarentola annularis),* fan-footed geckos *(Ptyodactylus hasselquistii),* *Stenodactylus* species, and microgeckos *(Tropiocolotes)* should be kept in desert vivaria with rockwork, dried wood sections, or cork bark. A section of moist substrate or a humidified shelter should be available. Create vertical rock areas or sections of cork bark for *Tarentola* and *Ptyodactylus.* Geckos require high calcium levels in their diet, particularly during the breeding season.

Anguidae (Legless Lizards, Alligator Lizards, Galliwasps)

This group includes species with many different requirements and adaptive constraints. The types of Anguidae available in herpetoculture can be grouped as legless lizards (*Anguis, Ophisaurus*), alligator lizards (*Abronia, Barisia, Elgaria, Gerrhonotus*), and galliwasps (*Diploglossus*). The most readily available and most easily maintained of the anguids are sheltopusiks (*Ophisaurus apodus*), commonly offered as giant legless lizards. They are opportunistic carnivores that will feed on insects, snails (one of their favorites), prekilled mice of the appropriate size, and dog or cat food.

Alligator lizards, with the exception of the members of the genus *Elgaria*, are best considered as species for specialists. The great majority of alligator lizards have not been successfully established. The southern alligator lizard, *Elgaria multicarinata*, is the most easily kept of the alligator lizards. It is easy to maintain in a vivarium with a sand, moss, and soil mix. One half of the vivarium should be kept dampened. Provide a shelter and climbing areas of cork bark. It enjoys temperatures in the high 70s to low 80s F (25°C to 28.3°C) during the day, with a 10-degree F

Alligator lizards (*Abronia graminea*) are best kept by specialists, who can meet their needs.

Shown is a Chinese legless lizard (*Ophisaurus hartii*).

(5.5-degree C) temperature drop at night. During the winter, southern alligator lizards should be hibernated with daytime temperatures in the 60s F (15.6°C to 20.6°C) and nighttime temperatures in the 50s F (10°C to 15°C). They will breed readily in the spring and will usually lay multiple clutches. Do not keep males together; they will fight.

Other species are challenging. For example, the impressive Texas alligator lizard, *Gerrhonotus infernalis*, the giant of the group (up to 20 inches), has yet to be established in captivity. Sensitivity to excessive D_3 supplementation may be one of the factors contributing to failure, but there may be additional factors to consider. Members of the genus *Barisia* vary in their adaptability to captive conditions. Most have a low tolerance for D_3 and few have been successfully established in captivity.

Like *Barisia*, most *Abronia* have not been successfully established in captivity. *Abronia* are considered the Cadillacs of anguids, with beautiful forms and intricate scalation and patterns. Most are cloud forest dwellers that require temperatures in the upper 70s (82°F maximum) during the day and significant night drops. They also need at least 70 percent relative humidity and good ventilation. They are sensitive to excessive supplementation, notably vitamin D_3, so they require a UVB source. When available, *Abronia* rank among the most expensive of the lizards.

Galliwasps (*Diploglossus*) are secretive semifossorial species that adapt reasonably well to captivity when adequate environmental conditions are provided. However, their secretive nature makes them poor displays, and the larger, more impressive, and colorful species such as *D. monotropis* can be flighty and aggressive, limiting their appeal to specialists.

Agamidae

Agamids are widely distributed Old World lizards that have successfully colonized a wide variety of habitats. The species most often offered in the pet trade are agamas (*Agama*), bearded dragons (*Pogona*), sailfin lizards (*Hydrosaurus*), and tree dragons (*Acanthosaura, Calotes, Gonocephalus*)

Agama species live primarily in arid to semi-arid areas. They should be kept in desert vivaria with rockwork and climbing areas. Many species do not fare well in captivity because they are specialized for feeding on ants. Others are more generalized feeders and adapt better to captivity. Many *Agama* species eat some vegetable matter, such as grated vegetables and chopped romaine, mustard greens, and flower petals. Exposure to sunlight or a UVB source is recommended. Provide a basking area that reaches a temperature of 90°F to 100°F (32.2°C to 37.8°C).

Many of the agamas, such as this blue-coated tree agama, prefer branches and rocks to climb on.

Much easier to keep under the same conditions mentioned above are the shield-tailed (*Xenagama taylori*) and turnip-tailed agamas (*Xenagama batillifera*). These require 2 to 3 inches of sandy soil for burrowing. Basking rocks and wood should be secured to prevent crushing the lizards should they burrow under them. Both species feed readily on supplemented insects, greens, and yellow flowers, and they do not appear to require a UVB source.

Green water dragons (*Physignathus cocincinus*) and sailfin lizards (*Hydrosaurus*) are some of the largest agamine lizards. They require large tropical vivaria with a sizeable water area. The water dragons are primarily insectivorous, but they also eat small mammals, dead animal foods (such as dog food), and some vegetable matter. Sailfin lizards have dietary requirements similar to those of water dragons except that they become more vegetarian by the time they are adults. Both are egg layers and do breed in captivity. Green water dragons can be kept in groups of one male and several females, but sailfin lizards should be kept only as single pairs.

The Australian *Pogona* species, known in the trade as bearded dragons, are among the most popular of the lizards. The inland bearded dragon (*Pogona vitticeps*) is the most readily available species. Several thousand are bred annually by hobbyists in the United States. They should be kept in

Sailfin lizards can be kept similarly to water dragons.

Despite being considered the most docile of captives, bearded dragons can still look ferocious when provoked.

desert vivaria with climbing areas of rock or cork rounds or dried wood sections. They are insectivorous but also eat vegetable matter, including mustard greens, kale, and flower petals. Expose bearded dragons to sunlight or a UVB bulb, particularly when raising juveniles. Sexing can be done through manual eversion of the hemipenes and through sexually dimorphic characteristics, including a relatively larger head and the presence of enlarged femoral and preanal pores in males. Bearded dragons breed readily and lay several clutches of up to twenty eggs per breeding season. The increasingly popular painted agamas (*Laudakia stellio brachydactyla*) can be kept under the same conditions.

In recent years, there has been increasing interest in a group generally called tree dragons, which includes *Acanthosaura* (mountain horned lizards), *Gonocephalus*, and *Calotes*. With the exception of mountain horned lizards, this group is considered challenging to keep long term and is recommended for more experienced keepers.

All tree dragons are tropical forest species that require a heat gradient with daytime background temperatures in the upper 70s F; the basking branches near a heat bulb should reach 90°F. Relative humidity should be 70 to 80 percent. This is best achieved by covering half of the screen top with plastic. A number of branches should be available for climbing. As a rule, it is best to keep the cage setups simple until specimens become established. They should be misted lightly once daily and offered a large shallow water dish. They will eat the standard insect fare, but you will have to experiment to find which type of insect is preferred by your individual lizard. Imports should be deparasitized if they show signs of weight loss. A UVB fluorescent bulb is recommended, but keepers have had good success keeping these species with light vitamin-mineral supplementation of insects and no UVB source.

Chameleonidae (True chameleons)

The true chameleons include the Madagascar leaf chameleons (*Brookesia*), the African pygmy chameleons (*Rampholeon*), Madagascar chameleons in the genus *Furcifer* (e.g. panther and Oustalet's chameleons, *F. pardalis* and *F. oustaleti*) and *Calumma* (e.g., Parson's chameleon, *C. parsonii*), African chameleons in the genera *Chamaeleo* (e.g. veiled chameleon, *C. calyptratus*), and *Bradypodion* (e.g., Fischer's chameleon, *B. fischeri*). Males have hemipenile bulges; there are also sexually dimorphic characteristics such as size, color, and enlarged helmets or ornaments in males.

Much needs to be learned about the best environmental and dietary parameters for multigenerational breeding and maintenance of chameleons. After more than twenty years of having dedicated herpetoculturists working with twenty different species of chameleons, only two—the veiled chameleon and the panther chameleon—have been firmly established as multigenerational, self-sustaining captive populations. Jackson's chameleons could rank as a third species, but inexpensive imports have derailed commercial breeding efforts, making it difficult to assess their captive status. Parson's chameleons are the longest lived of chameleons in captivity, but consistent breeding success has not yet been achieved. If all importation were to cease, at

A graceful chameleon (*Chamaeleo gracilis*) utilizes its prehensile tail on a tree branch.

best a handful of species (assuming last-ditch efforts were made to establish captive animals) would be likely to remain available in the trade.

Most chameleons are best kept singly except for breeding introductions. Some species can be kept in sexual pairs in larger enclosures. In spite of claims to the contrary, some species show a degree of sociability and even signs of temporary pair bonding.

A chameleon's basic requirements are simple to provide: a screen cage or a large and tall glass-sided tank with screen top, a small tree (*Ficus benjamina* is the most widely used), a basking light, and a UVB source. Relative humidity for most species is best at around 70 percent. Every one to two days, the lizards should be fed gut-loaded crickets of the appropriate size, superworms, and roaches (a favorite). Larger species may occasionally eat pink mice. All chameleons should be provided with a drip system as a source of water. They will not drink from water containers.

In terms of temperature, chameleons can be split into two groups: (1) species that like daytime temps into the upper 80s F and whose eggs will survive incubation at higher than 74°F, and (2) species whose maximum daytime temperature should be around 82°F and whose eggs will not survive incubation

The Parson's chameleon (*Calumma parsonii*) is the largest of the chameleon species.

temperatures above 74°F. Group 1 includes species such as the popular veiled chameleons, panther chameleons, Oustalet's chameleons, flap-necked chameleons, Senegal chameleons, and African chameleons (*Chamaeleo africanus*). Group 2 includes montium chameleons, four-horned chameleons, crested chameleons, Johnston's chameleons, and many live-bearing (ovoviviparous) chameleons.

To promote the synthesizing of vitamin D_3, use UVB-generating bulbs or provide your chameleon with at least six hours of exposure to sunlight on a weekly basis. There is some evidence that many species could obtain adequate amounts of vitamin D_3 through dietary supplementation; however, it is difficult to determine adequate dosage when supplementing with vitamin D_3. Some chameleons, notably small and slow-growing species, have proven sensitive to oversupplementation, which can be fatal. Because there has not been much methodical research on this topic in regard to chameleons, it is best to err on the side of caution and provide a UVB source. If you do offer a UVB source, reduce to no or very little D_3 supplementation.

Anyone wanting to keep chameleons should first try a hand with one of the two established species before tackling the ones with more stringent requirements. Remember that wild-collected chameleons are usually parasitized and should be treated accordingly. Although captive bred is generally better than wild caught, except in the case of the established chameleons, the babies of most species can be more difficult to raise and less likely to survive than wild-caught subadult to adults. This group of lizards is popular, and a great deal information can be found in specialist books and on the Internet.

Cordylidae (Girdle-Tailed Lizards)

The girdle-tailed lizards include several popular species in the genus *Cordylus* sold as armadillo lizards. The largest and most sought after is the giant sungazer (*C. giganteus*), which grows to just over 12 inches. Members of the girdle-tailed (*Cordylus*), false girdle-tailed (formerly *Pseudocordylus* but now placed in *Cordylus*), and flat lizards (*Platysaurus*) are hardy animals that are among the sturdiest of the lizards to keep in captivity. Some species are very colorful.

Girdle-tailed lizards should be set up in large desert vivaria with rockwork. Temperatures in the day should be in

Girdle-tailed lizards are often sold as armadillo lizards.

the 80s F (26.7°C to 31.7°C) with a basking spot. Nighttime temperatures should drop 10 to 15 degrees F (5.5 to 7.7 degrees C). By manipulating the temperature and photoperiod, many of these lizards will breed. Use a cooling regimen a few degrees colder than that used for subtropical lizards. They are live bearing with one to four young except *Platysaurus*. Because of relatively low reproductive rates, these species could be impacted by unmanaged commercial collecting. They are not recommended for handling.

Gerrhosauridae (Plated lizards)

Plated lizards rank among the easier to keep species and include the popular and docile Sudan (*Gerrhosaurus major*) and yellow-throated (*G. flavigularis*) plated lizards. In recent years, Madagascar plated lizards of the genus *Zonosaurus* have also become available. Most plated lizards are omnivorous and will eat some fruit and processed foods, such as dog food, in addition to insect fare.

Shown is a dwarf plated lizard (*Cordylosaurus subtessellatus*).

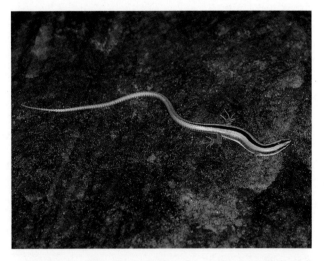

Members of the genus *Gerrhosaurus* (African) will do well in a desert or dry forest-type vivarium. The substrate should be dry except for one moistened area (soil, sand, and orchid bark mix) in a pan buried flush with the dry substrate. Generally, African plated lizards (*Gerrhosaurus*) are hardy and easy to keep. These lizards are egg layers.

Members of the genus *Zonosaurus* (Malagasy) can be kept in a vivarium with a soil, sand, and fine orchid bark mixture as a substrate. Half of the substrate in the enclosure should be kept dry, and half should be kept slightly moist. Success has also been had keeping *Zonosaurus* species on orchid bark and keeping some species, such as *Z. quadrilineatus*, on sand. The larger species are easier to keep than the smaller ones. Males have large femoral pores. They are egg layers.

Corytophanidae (Casque-headed lizards)

This group includes basilisks (*Basiliscus*), helmeted iguanids (*Corytophanes*), and cone-head lizards (*Laemanctus*). There are three species of basilisks regularly available in the trade: *B. basiliscus, B. plumifrons,* and *B. vittatus.* The first two species are bred in some numbers in captivity. They require large tropical vivaria. Because of their arboreal habits, provide plants. They need large water containers and shelters in the form of sections of cork tube. They are easy to breed. The biggest problem with the basilisks is skittish flight behavior, sometimes leading to smashed snouts. Males should be kept separately. They are egg layers, usually laying two to three clutches per year.

This young male green basilisk (*Basiliscus plumifrons*) was found in Costa Rica.

The helmeted iguanid or forest chameleon (*Corytophanes cristatus*) is a neat arboreal species that tends to be difficult in the long term and is not recommended for beginners. It requires a warm, planted tropical vivarium with branches or cork rounds, moderately high relative humidity, and adequate ventilation. Imports should be treated for parasites. These animals should not be handled except when necessary. A drip watering system is a good idea. They are insectivorous and egg laying.

Cone-head lizards (*Laemanctus*) can be kept under the same conditions as helmeted iguanids and tend to be easier to keep long term and successfully breed.

Crotaphytinae (North American Collared Lizards and Leopard Lizards)

Collared and leopard lizards are characterized by their large heads, long hind limbs, and the ability to run bipedally. Male collared lizards tend to be more colorful and larger than females and show hemipenile bulges. They also tend to develop larger heads. Gravid females develop bright orange blotches along their sides. Some of the morphs of collared lizards (*Crotaphytus*) are arguably the most beautiful of the North American lizards and have attracted a small following of specialists. These attractive lizards are now being captive bred in small numbers in the United States.

Shown are a female collared lizard (*Crotaphytus collaris*) (right) and a male collared lizard (left).

The collared lizards and leopard lizards are known for their ability to run bipedally.

Captive-bred animals are very adaptable and tame lizards that many consider personable. These will fare well in large desert vivaria. Temperatures during the day should be in the 80s F (26.7°C to 31.7°C), with a basking spot in the 90s F (32.2°C to 37.2°C) at the area closest to the light. Night temperatures can drop into the 60s F (15.6°C to 20.6°C) during most of the year and into the 50s F (10°C to 15°C) during the winter. Provide rocks and shelters and areas for climbing, such as section of cork round. These lizards are diggers, so rocks must be anchored firmly and care taken to protect the bases of plants when designing a naturalistic vivarium. Use a UVB light for these species. These lizards are egg layers and will breed readily following winter cooling and reduced photoperiod.

Lacertidae

Thirty genera of Old World lizards belong to this family. The ones most often offered in herpetoculture are green and jeweled lacertas (*Lacerta viridis* and *Timon lepidus*), wall lizards (*Podarcis*), long-tailed grass lizards (*Takydromus*), and more recently the diminutive but beautiful African blue-tailed tree lizard (*Holaspis guntheri*). Of the imported lacertides from Europe and North Africa (*Acanthodactylus, Lacerta,* and *Podarcis*), some of the most impressive species are the eyed or jewel lacerta *(Lacerta lepida)* and the green lacerta (*Lacerta viridis*).

Most of the European and North African imported lacertides will fare best in desert-type vivaria with rockwork and shelters. If kept too damp, some species will develop a skin disease that often proves fatal. They are best kept in groups of one male with several females. The larger species may attack other lizards, particularly males, during breeding. Otherwise, many of the species are quite hardy and entertaining vivarium animals. They are primarily insectivorous, although they do eat some plant matter and soft fruit. *Lacerta* and *Podarcis* breed readily following winter cooling. They are egg laying except for the viviparous lizard (*Lacerta vivipara*). Males typically have enlarged femoral pores. Lacertids may also be sexually dimorphic, the males often being larger, with larger heads and, in some cases, brighter coloration.

The long-tailed grass lizard (*Takydromus* sp.) is the only one of the Asian lacertids that is regularly imported.

Long-tailed grass lizards (*Takydromus*) are the only regularly imported Asian lacertids. They will fare best in a half-dry, half-moist vivarium with a substrate of orchid bark and potting soil. Provide twigs and low plants for climbing. Small one- to two-week-old crickets should be offered as food.

The green lacerta (*Lacerta viridis*) is considered one of the most beautiful lacertids.

Make water in a shallow container available at all times. They should be kept in the high 70s F (25°C to 26°C) with a low-wattage basking light. Night temperatures can drop into the 60s F (15.6°C to 20.6°C). They are egg laying.

Oplurinae (Malagasy Iguanids)

This group is now considered by some as deserving family status, the Opluridae. It includes the species *Chalarodon madagascariensis* and several species in the genus *Oplurus*. The most readily available species are *O. cuvieri* and *O. cyclurus*. These look like giant swifts with spiky tails.

They are best kept in desert vivaria with some rockwork and possibly a section of cholla, dry wood, or cork. Unlike many other lizard species, they do not autotomize (drop) their tails. They are primarily insectivorous. They are egg layers, usually with small clutches (four to six eggs) laid between rocks.

The Malagasy iguanids (*Chalarodon madagascariensis*) are now considered by some as a separate family, the Opluridae.

Phrynosomatinae

This subfamily includes the popular swifts (*Sceloporus*), horned lizards (*Phrynosoma*), and Baja blue rock lizards (*Petrosaurus thalassinus*). Horned lizards rank among the most appealing of all desert species. Unfortunately, they require exacting conditions and a diet that includes certain species of ants to fare well long term. Most species are also subject to varying degrees of legal protection. All of these factors make them suitable only for dedicated specialists attempting to establish and breed these species in captivity before wild-collected specimens are no longer legally available. Although horned lizards can be maintained under the same conditions as many desert species, their dietary requirement for certain ants creates a husbandry constraint that has killed tens of thousands of these lizards. They are among the most difficult lizards to keep. On the bright side, in recent years, a small number of Internet businesses have offered harvester ants, a species relished by most horned lizards. These can be ordered as needed.

The Texas horned lizard is capable of squirting blood from its eyes as a defensive posture.

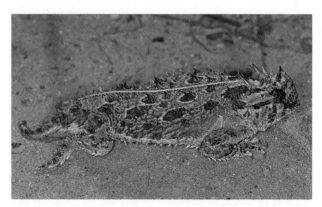

The basic requirements for horned lizards are a short tank at least 30 inches long for adults, a sandy substrate, a basking area where temperatures reach 100°F to 105°F (38°C to 40.5°C), and a UVB source. Although they are desert lizards, they should be offered water two to three times a week through misting and should have a shallow water container at all times. Ants should make up at least 50 percent of their diet. They can also be fed supplemented small crickets and mealworms. There are now a small number of Internet forums and sites dedicated to this group of lizards. It can't be emphasized enough that you must research the species and its requirements before making a purchase.

Spiny lizards (*Sceloporus*) are the most readily available of the phrynosomatids. Most of the U.S. species offered in the trade can be kept in desert vivaria with rock and wood in the landscape. They require warm temperatures during the day with a significant drop at night. Winter cooling is required for breeding. Primarily insectivorous, they will also eat plant matter. Exposure to sunlight or a UVB source is recommended. *Sceloporus* includes both egg-laying and live-bearing species. Occasionally imported from Central America, the emerald swift (*Sceloporus malachitus*) fares better in a tropical vivarium. Provide cork sections for it to climb on.

Polychrotinae (Anoles and Prehensile-Tailed Iguanids)

This subfamily includes the anoles, chameleon anoles, and the prehensile-tailed species in the genus *Polychrus*. Anoles (*Anolis*) are among the most popular lizard species, particularly the green anole. They fare well in planted tropical vivaria. Some species live on bark; others prefer to be at ground level. Relative humidity requirements vary somewhat among species. Most species are arboreal, requiring branches for climbing. They are insect eating but also eat

Shown is a male Yarrow's spiny lizard.

banana baby food and certain soft fruit. They are best kept in groups of one male with several females. Water should be provided through misting or a water-drip system. They are egg laying, typically with one egg per clutch. Males have hemipenile bulges. In anoles, males are often larger, with larger heads and with dewlaps.

The green anole isn't the only anole worth keeping. Shown is the knight anole.

Scincidae (Skinks)

Skinks number more than 1,000 species and are probably the most abundant of the lizards. It is not possible to make broad generalizations for this group. As a rule, skinks from forests with moist soils should be kept in a forest floor vivarium, with a burrowing medium consisting of a soil, fine orchid bark, and sand mixture. Provide cork sections for shelters and climbing areas. Skinks from desert areas usually fare well on sand. Provide rock and sections of bark for climbing and basking. Some desert-burrowing species, such as the sandfish (*Scincus*) and many of the barrel skinks (*Chalcides*), fare well only if kept on sand. Sexing can be difficult with many species, although manual eversion of the hemipenes often works if applied gently. In some species, sexual dimorphism, including larger head size, more coloration, and broader tail base in males, can be used for sexing.

The blue tongue skink is one of the best known of the skinks.

In addition to eating insects, many of the small to medium skinks will feed on dog food as well as some fruits and vegetables. Some of the larger skinks, such as the prehensile-tailed skink, are primarily vegetarian.

Teiidae (Ameivas, Tegus, Caiman Lizards, Whiptails, and Racerunners)

The popular large tegus, ameivas, and tropical whiptail lizards belong to this family. Tegus have requirements similar to the larger monitor lizards and will not be covered here. Ameivas are occasionally imported in some numbers, as are certain tropical whiptail lizards (*Cnemidophorus*). They are best kept in large vivaria with a thick layer of a sand and peat moss or a sand and potting soil mix. The substrate should be slightly dampened and patted down so that it is cohesive enough to allow for digging of burrows. You can also insert sections of PVC pipe at an angle in the substrate. One section should contain mulch or a pile of leaves for the ameivas and tropical whiptails to burrow in.

These species like warm (85°F [29.4°C]) daytime temperatures. A spotlight should be provided, as well as some diversity of landscape through rockwork or, preferably, sections of wood or cork. The relative humidity for tropical species should be around 70 percent. The vivarium should have good ventilation. Provide a UVB source, either sunlight, a

mercury vapor UVB lamp, or UVB fluorescent bulbs. These lizards are insectivorous but will also feed on lean meat strips. They will also eat some soft fruit and cooked mashed vegetables. Desert teiids, such as desert whiptail lizards, are best kept in desert vivaria with shelters and dry leaf piles. Provide sunlight or another UVB source.

Varanidae (Monitor Lizards)

Monitor lizards consist of about 60 species in the genus *Varanus,* which includes ten subgenera. They range from the foot-long short-tailed monitor (*V. brevicauda*) to the gigantic Komodo dragon (*V. komodoensis*), which can reach 9 feet (2.7 m) and is the largest of the living lizards. I will not cover the larger popular species, as these require room-size enclosures and are unsuitable pets for the majority of people.

In recent years, dwarf and small monitor species have become available. They can be kept and bred in moderately large vivaria with a floor space of only 8 to 12 square feet (4 ft x 2 ft to 6 ft x 2 ft). Most of these species are the dwarf members of the subgenus *Odatria* (ridge-tailed, Timor, Kimberly Rock, freckled, Pilbara monitors, and others). Several of the smaller monitors are now being bred in captivity.

Provide a basking site that reaches up to 130°F right beneath the heat bulb. The outer areas of the vivarium should be in the upper 70s. The dwarf monitors like to dig and burrow; use a soil or soil and sand mix that is kept slightly moist so that the upper layer dries and the lower layer retains moisture. Provide shelters and secure climbing areas. UVB is not required for successfully keeping these monitors. Offer them plenty of food in the form of insects and pink or fuzzy mice. There is a great deal information now available on the care of these species.

Although some monitors make good captives, many are quite ferocious.

Other small monitors suitable for vivarium care and breeding are the green, black, and blue tree monitors (*Varanus prasinus*, *V. beccari*, and *V. macraei*). They require enclosures at least 4 ft long x 2 ft wide x 6 ft high. Use a soil substrate that is kept moist. Provide climbing branches, aboveground shelters, and a heat source with temperatures in the 90s F near the basking light. Daytime background temperature should be in the upper 70s to low 80s F (25°C to 28.3°C). Relative humidity should be 80 to 90 percent and is best maintained by offering water in a large shallow container. UVB light is recommended. Feed insects and small mice.

SOME USEFUL HERPETOCULTURAL TERMS

Herpetoculturists use certain terms to describe the habits or requirements of various lizard species. The following terms are commonly used to describe the behaviors of lizards:

arboreal: living or active on trees and shrubs, e.g., knight anoles (*Anolis equestris*) and true chameleons (*Chamaeleo*)

crepuscular: active at dawn or twilight

diurnal: active during the daytime

fossorial: living or active at least part of the time in a substrate such as soil or sand, e.g., sand fish (*Scincus scincus*) and ocellated skinks (*Chalcides ocellatus*)

nocturnal: active at night

saxicolous: living or active among rocks, e.g., Baja blue rock lizard (*Petrosaurus thalassinus*) and cordylids

semi-aquatic: living or active part of the time in water, e.g., crocodile lizards (*Shinisaurus crocodilurus*) and Asian water skinks (*Tropidophorus*)

semi-arboreal: living or active on trees and shrubs part of the time, e.g., bearded dragons (*Pogona vitticeps*) and green water dragons (*Physignathus cocincinus*)

terrestrial: living or active on the ground surface, e.g., leopard geckos (*Eublepharis macularius*) and curly-tailed lizards (*Leiocephalus*)

Herpetoculturists use the following arbitrary terms to group lizards according to climatic and vivarium requirements:

montane: inhabiting mountain or high-altitude areas. Herpetoculturists, by adding the term *montane* to the descriptive terms above, indicate that because the species lives in a high altitude, it has special temperature requirements, either cooler nights or generally cooler temperatures. This usually implies that species will not fare well long term under a standard warm temperature regimen.

subtropical: inhabiting areas adjacent to the tropics. In terms of herpetoculture, this means lizard species that require warmth during most of the year; they should be exposed to moderately warm daytime temperatures, cooler nights, and a reduced photoperiod in the winter.

temperate: inhabiting either the North Temperate Zone between the Arctic Circle and the Tropic of Cancer or the South Temperate Zone between the Antarctic Circle and the Tropic of Capricorn. In terms of herpetoculture, this refers to lizards exposed to seasonal variations in temperature, including warm summers and cool to cold winters. Hibernation (brumation) is generally recommended for these species to breed and to fare well long term in captivity. Temperate lizards are also subject to annual variations in day length, with long days in the summer and short days in the winter.

tropical: inhabiting the tropics. There are many life zones in the tropics, and no generalization can be made on lizard species from tropical areas. Thus, it is critical that keepers obtain additional information on tropical species. If a lizard is a montane species, it may be subject to slightly warm daytime temperatures and cool, possibly cold, nights. At one time, lack of information regarding the life zones of several species of montane chameleons (including the popular Jackson's chameleon) led to poor husbandry methods that resulted in their being difficult to keep in captivity.

Herpetoculturists normally use the term *tropical* when referring to species from lowland tropical areas, usually moist tropical forest species rather than dry tropical forest species. The former usually fare well in tropical forest floor or tropical forest vivaria; the latter usually fare well in desert vivaria. Species from lowland tropical forests typically require warm daytime temperatures in the mid- to high 80s F (26.7°C to 31.7°C) and mild nighttime temperatures in the high 70s to low 80s F (25°C to 28.3°C). Relative humidity tends to be high in lowland tropical forest habitats.

APPENDIX II

AN OVERVIEW OF LIZARD FAMILIES AND SUBFAMILIES

Because systematics is undergoing great change as a result of DNA analysis, the following is a general guide based on one currently used system of classification. The listed subfamilies are not recognized by all herpetologists. Examples of species sold in the trade are listed when applicable.

Order: Squamata
  Suborder: Sauria
    Infraorder: Iguania
      Family: Agamidae
        Subfamily: *Agaminae*: agamas, dragons, sailfin lizards
        Subfamily: *Leiolepidinae*: uromastyx, butterfly agamas
      Family: Chamaeleonidae (true chameleons)
        Subfamily: *Brookesiinae* (dwarf and leaf chameleons)
        Subfamily: *Chamaeleoninae* (chameleons)
      Family: Iguanidae
        Subfamily: *Corytophanidae* (basilisks, conehead lizards, helmeted iguanids)
        Subfamily: *Crotaphytidae* (collared lizards, leopard lizards)
        Subfamily: *Hoplocercinae* (club-tailed iguanas)

Subfamily: *Iguaninae* (green iguana, spiny-tailed iguana)
Subfamily: *Oplurinae* (Madagascar iguanas)
Subfamily: *Phrynosomatidae* (horned lizards, spiny lizards)
Subfamily: *Polychrotidae* (anoles, prehensile-tailed iguanids [bush anoles])
Subfamily: *Tropidurinae* (curly-tailed lizards, lava lizards, South American swifts)
Suborder: Scleroglossa
Infraorder: Gekkota
Family: Eublepharidae (geckos with movable eyelids)
Family: Diplodactylidae (Australian, New Caledonian, New Zealand endemic geckos, e.g., knob-tailed geckos (*Nephrurus*); giant geckos (*Rhacodactylus*); eyelash geckos (*Strophurus*)
Family: Gekkonidae (geckos with immovable eyelids)
Subfamily: *Sphaerodactylinae* (New World day geckos, *Gonatodes, Sphaerodactylus*)
Subfamily: *Gekkoninae* (house geckos [*Hemidactylus*] and tokay geckos)
Family: Pygopodidae (legless geckos)
Infraorder: Scincomorpha
Family: Cordylidae (armadillo lizards, girdle-tailed lizards, sungazers)
Family: Cordylidae (armadillo lizards, girdle
Family: Gerrhosauridae (plated lizards)
Subfamily: *Gerrhosaurinae* (African plated lizards)
Subfamily: *Zonosaurinae* (Madagascar plated lizards)
Family: Gymnophthalmidae (spectacled lizards)

Family: Lacertidae
  Subfamily: *Gallotiinae* (*Gallotia*, Canary
      Islands lacertids)
  Subfamily: *Lacertinae* (Lacertas, fringe-
      toed lacertids)
Family: Scincidae (skinks)
  Subfamily: *Scincinae* (barrel skinks
      [*Chalcides*], U.S. skinks
      [*Eumeces*], sandfish [*Scincus*])
  Subfamily: *Acontinae* (South African leg-
      less skinks)
  Subfamily: *Feyliniinae* (not readily avail-
      able African species)
  Subfamily: *Lygosominae* (many of the
      popular species including
      Mabuya, Tiliqua, and
      Tribolonotus)
Family: Teiidae
  Subfamily: *Teiinae* (ameivas, whiptail and
      rainbow lizards)
  Subfamily: *Tupinambinae* (tegus, Cayman
      lizards)
Family: Xantusiidae (night lizards [*Xantusia,*
      Lepidophyma])
Family: Anguidae
  Subfamily: *Anguinae*: legless lizards,
      sheltopusik
  Subfamily: *Anniellinae*: western legless
      lizards
  Subfamily: *Diploglossinae*: galliwasps
  Subfamily:*Gerrhonotinae*: alligator lizards
Family: Xenosauridae (crocodile lizards,
      xenosaurs)
Infraorder: Varanoidea
  Family: Helodermatidae (Gila monster, beaded
      lizards)
  Family: Lanthanotidae (earless monitor)
  Family: Varanidae (monitor lizards)

APPENDIX III

REHOMING LIZARDS

There may be a time in your life when you find you are unable to continue to care for your animals. Life changes, such as going away to school, moving, and changes in family structure, can leave you unable to continue to keep your animals. The first course of action in such a situation is to find out if there are friends or other hobbyists who might be interested in the animals you own. Advertising in herpetological society newsletters or in the pet section of the classified ads of your newspaper may help you find interested buyers. If you are in a hurry, the easiest course is to sell your animals back to the store where you purchased them or to make arrangements over the phone to sell them to one of the many specialty reptile dealers. Remember that dealers will usually pay a wholesale price for animals, approximately one-half to one-third of the price a customer will pay for them (stores have many expenses, and the prices paid for the animals take into account such factors as rent, employee wages, insurance, cost of maintaining animals, and profit). If you cannot sell your animals, consider giving them to a store, herpetological society adoption committee or auction, or the science department of a local school.

Do not under any circumstances release your animals into the wild. The release of nonnative species into the wild can jeopardize native wildlife as well as our rights as herpetoculturists to keep nonnative species. For all our sakes, and for the sake of the animals, do not ever do this. Resorting to the recourses mentioned above, you should be able to find alternative homes for your animals.

APPENDIX IV

PRODUCTS

Note: The author has chosen not to list the addresses of manufacturers listed in this manual: first, because most do not sell direct to the public; and second, because the products are available through retail sources, either stores or mail order. Check the manufacturers' Web sites and advertisers in herpetocultural magazines or Internet reptile/herpetoculture portals for sources.

Calcium Carbonate

This is sometimes available in feed stores under the name of limestone flour. It should be more readily available in the reptile trade named simply calcium carbonate or oyster shell calcium.

Calcium/D$_3$ Supplements

Miner-all: A popular supplement made of fine-powdered calcium and 50 other minerals and trace minerals. Comes in a formula with D$_3$ (indoor) and without (outdoor or UVB source)

Rep Cal: A popular oyster shell calcium and vitamin D$_3$ supplement; a popular and readily available calcium-vitamin D$_3$ source; fine powdered and adheres well

T-Rex: Calcium powder and calcium-phosphorus supplements

Heating Equipment

Exo-Terra (a division of Hagen): A wide range of heating equipment

Flexwatt: Heat tape

Pearlco: Infrared heat emitters and panels

T-Rex: Heat bulbs, subtank heat pads, UVB heat

Zoo Med: A wide range of heating equipment, including heat bulbs, ceramic infrared emitters, hot rocks, and reptile heat pads

Hygrometers

Several reptile supply distributors now offer inexpensive stick-on hygrometers and digital hygrometers that are accurate enough for the purpose of keeping reptiles.

Lights

Exo-Terra: Various incandescent and UV-generating reptile bulbs.

T-Rex: Heat lights and mercury vapor UVB

Zoo Med: A wide range of reptile lighting, including heat bulbs, fluorescent UVB, and mercury vapor UVB

Scales

Edmund Scientific: A good source for relatively inexpensive yet accurate digital scales

Thermometers, Temperature Guns, and Thermostats

Alife: Offers a good basic thermostatic control

Helix Controls: An early pioneer in reptile thermostatic controls that offers a variety of temperature controllers, including pulse proportional thermostats and infrared temperature guns

Pro-Exotics: A range of infrared temperature guns, one of the essential tools of herpers

Pro-Products: Infrared temperature guns

Zoo Med: Digital thermometers, rheostats, and thermostats

Vitamin-Mineral Supplements

Mardel Laboratories: Produces vitamin-mineral supplements and some reptile health products

Rep-Cal: Manufacturer of Herptivite, a popular fine-powdered multivitamin supplement with beta-carotene and no formed A; to be used in combination with the company's calcium or calcium/D$_3$ powder

Tetra Terrafauna: Produces calcium and vitamin-mineral supplements

T-Rex: Offers an outstanding line of dusts for various herps, carefully formulated to balance the nutritional value of insects when used at every feeding

Zoo Med: Produces Reptivite, a powdered vitamin-mineral supplement popular among lizard keepers, as well as a range of reptile foods

Note: These lists reflect the author's information base on the major brands sold in the pet trade and are not intended to endorse specific products.

RESOURCES

Books

Alberts, A. 1994. "Ultraviolet Light and Lizards: More than Meets the Eye." *The Vivarium* 5 (4): 24–28. *Recommended reading for anyone trying to figure out what the UVA and UVB issue is all about.*

*De Vosjoli, P. 1992. *The General Care and Maintenance of Green Anoles.* Lakeside, CA: Advanced Vivarium Systems, Inc.

———— 1992. *The General Care and Maintenance of Green Water Dragons, Basilisks and Sailfin Lizards.* Lakeside, CA: Advanced Vivarium Systems, Inc.

*De Vosjoli, P. and R. Mailloux. 1993. *The General Care and Maintenance of Bearded Dragons.* Lakeside, CA: Advanced Vivarium Systems, Inc.,

*Frost, D. R. and R. Etheridge. 1989. A Phylogenetic Analysis and Taxonomy of Iguanian Lizards. Misc. Pub. No. 81 University of Kansas, Museum of Natural History, Lawrence, KS. *This work has generated quite a bit of controversy among taxonomists, but the methodology and taxonomic analysis are of the highest standards.*

*Frye, F. 1991. *Biomedical and Surgical Aspects of Reptile Husbandry.* Malabar, FL: Krieger. *This massive two-volume set established the foundation for reptile veterinary medicine. Although some information, such as drug dosages, is outdated, this impressive groundbreaking work remains a primary reference for anyone involved in the field of reptile medicine.*

*Frye, F. 1993. *Reptile Clinician's Handbook.* Malabar, FL: Krieger. *For the hobbyist, this small-format wire-bound*

book is a lot more user friendly and economical than the large two-volume set. It lacks photos, which are invaluable in helping the inexperienced hobbyist diagnose a lizard's condition. Metabolic bone disease, one of the most common problems in captive reptiles, is only briefly mentioned in this abridged work.

*Gehrmann, W. H. 1994. Spectral Characteristics of Lamps Commonly Used in Herpetoculture. *The Vivarium* 5 (5) 16–21. *A great article for anyone interested in lighting and reptile care. Highly recommended.*

Klingenberg, R. 2007. *Understanding Reptile Parasites.* Irvine, CA: Advanced Vivarium Systems. *Essential information every keeper should know about reptile parasites. This is the new revised and updated edition of the original 1993 bestseller. Highly recommended.*

Mader. D. R., ed. 2006. *Reptile Medicine and Surgery*, 2nd ed. Burlington, MA: W. B. Saunders. *This 1,000+ page book is considered the current primary reference on the subject. Invaluable for serious herpers.*

Marquardt, K., M. Levine, and M. La Rochelle. 1993. *Animal Scam: The Beastly Abuse of Human Rights.* Washington DC: Regnery Gateway. *Recommended for anyone interested in a different interpretation of animal rights organizations. This book exposes the not-so-ethical side of the people who are actively trying to put an end to the keeping of animals in captivity.*

*Mattison, C. 1991. *Keeping and Breeding Lizards.* London: Blandford, distributed by Sterling, New York. *This is a well-written overview of lizards and their herpetoculture.*

McKeown, S. 1993. *The General Care and Maintenance of Day Geckos.* Lakeside, CA: Advanced Vivarium Systems, Inc. *The standard English language reference on the herpetoculture of these popular lizards.*

*Rogner. M. 1997. *Lizards I and Lizards II.* Melbourne, FL: Krieger. *A must-have two-volume set for serious hobbyists that provides detailed herpetocultural information on a variety of species based on the work of European herpeto-cultutrists. Along with Zimmerman's work below, this is one of the great works of herpetoculture.*

*Zimmerman, E. 1986. *Breeding Terrarium Animals.* Neptune City, NJ: T.F.H. *An invaluable reference on keeping and breeding amphibians and reptiles. A gem of a book that should be in every lizard keeper's library. T.F.H. has republished this book with a different cover and title,* Reptiles and Amphibians: Care, Breeding and Behavior (1993).

*Zug, G. R., J. P. Caldwell, and L. J. Vitt. 2001. *Herpetology: An Introductory Biology of Amphibians and Reptiles,* 2nd ed. Burlington, MA: Academic Press. *A very readable and informative introduction to herpetology. Basic information all herpetoculturists and amateur herpetologists should know.*

*For information only; these resources are not cited in text.

Magazines/Bulletins

Reptiles Magazine
3 Burroughs
Irvine, CA 92618
949-855-8822
http://www.reptilesmagazine.com

Reptilia: The European Herp Magazine
Bisbe Urquinaona, 34 08860. Castelldefels (Barcelona) Spain
Tel: +34932050120
http://www.info@reptilia.net

Reptiles Care
Mulberry Publications, Ltd.
Suite 209, Wellington House,
Butt Road, Colchester Essex, CO3 3DA
United Kingdom

Bulletin of the Chicago Herpetological Society
2001 North Clark Street
Chicago, Illinois 60614
http://www.chicagoherp.org
This is one of the most popular and informational of the herpetological society publications. Some herpetological societies publish sizable and informative publications; others have an intersociety newsletter exchange program. Examine newsletters and bulletins to find those to which you would like to subscribe.

INDEX

surface-to-volume ratios, 49
sustained field culture, 7–8
swellings, 151
swifts (*Sceloporus*), 13, 130,
144–45, 182–83

T
tail dropping, 32
tails, 12, 31, 152–53
taxonomy, 191–93
tegus, 185–86
Teiidae family (*Teiinae* and
Tupinambinae), 24, 130,
185–86, 193
temperate lizards, 54, 55, 84,
89–90, 189
temperature, 46, 48, 83–85
terminology, 188–90
terrestrial-arboreal, defining, 188
terrestrial lizards: about, 162–66,
188; basking area for, 69, 76;
curly-tailed, 22; handling,
135; humidity for, 148; temperature, 78–79, 91; vivaria
for, 47, 58–59, 66; water container, 133
Texas horned lizard, 182
thermal gradient, 40, 46
thermometers, 86–87
thermoregulation, 46
thermostats, 86
ticks and mites, 39, 40, 143–46
Timor monitors (*Varanus timorensis*), 24
toad-headed agama
(*Phrynocephalus mystaceus*),
21, 24, 110, 118
toe pads, 12–13
Tokay gecko (*Gecko gecko*), 20, 111
tongue flicking, 13–14
tree dragons (*Gonocephalus* and
Calotes), 20, 24
tropical forest vivaria, 54–55, 85
tropical lizards, 189–90
Tropiocolotes geckos, 27
true chameleons (*Chamaeleo,
Furcifer, Brookesia* and
Rampholeon): about, 21, 24,
172–75, 189; and ant threats,
65; captive breeding, 5, 8, 25,
172–73; difficulty caring for,
16, 45; dwarfs, 26–27, 172;
feeding, 13, 113; humidity for,
101–3; in old age, 44; and parasites, 144, 146–47; temperature for, 89; and vitamin
supplements, 123, 125, 148;
vivaria for, 47, 55, 57, 58–59,
60; water in droplets for, 133.
See also specific species

U
UVA and UVB lighting, 94–96,
122, 174–75

V
Varanoidea family, 193. *See also*
monitors
veiled chameleon (*Chamaeleo
calyptratus*), 8, 13, 21, 24, 25
ventilation, 104–5
veterinarians, 141–43
vitamin-mineral supplementation, 49, 95, 121–27, 132, 148,
174–75
vivaria design: about, 13, 40,
63–64; landscaping, 65–66;
naturalistic, 70–73; shelters
and hide boxes, 66–69;
substrates, 64–65. *See also*
enclosures
vivaria types, 51–56, 84, 85
viviparous lizard (*Lacerta
vivipara*), 180

W
wall lizards (*Podarcis*), 23, 61–62,
180
water, 48, 55, 133–34
water dragon (*Physignathus
cocincinus*), 20; king mealworms and mice diet, 111;
vivaria for, 55
water skinks (*Tropidophorus*), 55
wax worms, 111–12
weight loss or gain, 38, 40, 47,
106, 152–53
whiptail lizards
(*Cnemidophorus*), 24,
185–86
wild-caught lizards, 24–25, 38,
175
wind coolers, 91–92
wingless fruit flies, 113
wire mesh enclosures, 58

Y
Yarrow's spiny lizard (*Sceloporus
jarrovi*), 183
yellow-throated plated lizard
(*Gerrhosaurus flavigularis*),
176–77

Z
Zonosaurus. *See* plated lizards
Zoological Record, 12

ABOUT THE AUTHOR

Philippe de Vosjoli was born in 1949 in Paris, France. When in his teens, he was introduced to naturalistic vivarium design by an eccentric former keeper at the Jardin des Plantes. Since that time, he has become a herpetocultural pioneer. He founded the first nationally distributed reptile and amphibian magazine, *The Vivarium*, and the best-selling *Advanced Vivarium Systems* line of reptile care books. His articles and books helped establish many of the standards used in the field today, including popularizing terms such as *herpetoculture* and *vivarium*.

In 1995, he was awarded the Josef Laszlo Memorial Award for Excellence in Herpetoculture for his contribution to the advancement of the field. He is currently working on developing a systems approach to keeping amphibians and reptiles that focuses on the aesthetic and functional aspects of naturalistic vivaria.